STON[] JACK[] HOUSE

Jonathan Reynolds

BROADWAY PLAY PUBLISHING INC
56 E 81st St., NY NY 10028-0202
212 772-8334 fax: 212 772-8358
http://www.BroadwayPlayPubl.com

STONEWALL JACKSON'S HOUSE
© Copyright 1997 by Jonathan Reynolds

First printing: December 1997
ISBN: 0-88145-140-1

Book design: Marie Donovan
Word processing: Microsoft Word for Windows
Typographic controls: Xerox Ventura Publisher 2.0 PE
Typeface: Palatino
Copy editing: Liam Brosnahan
Printed on recycled acid-free paper and bound in the USA

PLAYS BY JONATHAN REYNOLDS

FIGHTING INTERNATIONAL FAT
GENIUSES
STYNE AFTER STYNE *(libretto)*
WHOOPEE! *(adaptation of a libretto)*
TUNNEL FEVER or THE SHEEP IS OUT
ESCAPE *(a play for television)*
YANKS 3 DETROIT 0 TOP OF THE 7TH *(one-act)*
RUBBERS *(one-act)*

for
William O Brasmer
Professor of Theater Arts, Denison University

Wynn Handman
Artistic Director, American Place Theater

Two Inspiring Water-Roilers

STONEWALL JACKSON'S HOUSE premiered at the
American Place Theater (Wynn Handman, Artistic
Director; Susannah Halston, Executive Director) on
17 February 1997. The cast and creative contributors
were:

LAWANDA .... Lisa Louise Langford
JUNIOR .... R E Rodgers
MAG .... Katherine Leask
BARNEY .... Ron Faber
DEL .... Mimi Bensinger

Director .... Jamie Richards
Scenic design .... Henry S Dunn
Lighting design .... Chad McArver
Costume design .... Barbara A Bell
Sound design .... Kurt B Kellenberger
Casting .... Rebecca Taichman
Production stage manager .... Joe Witt
Production supervisor .... Jonathan Morrison

Note:during the run of the play, the role of LAWANDA *was
also played by* Starla Benford.

CHARACTERS & SETTING

LAWANDA GAYLE. Nineteen to twenty-three and daydreamy, costumed as a middle-class Confederate housewife, which is customary for a guide—except that LAWANDA is black and there were few middle-class blacks in the Confederacy.

BARNEY GOSHEN. Fifty-five to sixty-five, married to DEL, with a rich, seductive baritone voice and an extremely kind face and manner. Also wears classically tasteful clothing.

DEL GOSHEN. Fifty to sixty, a genteel WASP from Ohio with a soothing voice and calming demeanor. She wears classically tasteful clothing.

JUNIOR NUCKOLLS. Twenty-five to forty, married to MAG, also from the Deep South, and quick to lose his temper. In the north, he would be called a redneck. He might wear a straw cowboy hat, and sideburns.

MAG NUCKOLLS. Twenty-five to forty, opinionated, angry at the world, and from the Deep South. She carries two cameras, and her hair is highly teased.

The same actors also play the following characters:

TRACY MUNSON. Twenty-five, black, attractive, middle-class with trendy clothes. She is a grad student at N Y U, extremely articulate and passionate. She has no other life but her job.

OZ O'CONNELL. Sixty-five. Feisty, opinionated, wise, highly respected in his field, and devoted to his wife GABRIELLA.

GABRIELLA KOHNER. Sixty-four. A bravura, committed actress, with a surreal way of expressing herself. Easily indignant, she and her husband have been social activists since the forties.

CLAIRE HENNOCK. Twenty-five to thirty-five, British, and alternately cold and sensual. A keen sense of history, men, and the heart of an argument.

JOE ROCK. Thirty-four. An angry young man without much money.

The action takes place in the house once lived in by Stonewall Jackson in Lexington, Virginia, and in the rehearsal room of a not-for-profit theater. The rooms of the house are decorated true to the period of 1863, the year Jackson died (or as described in the play). Each has a velvet rope across its doorway to protect it from misbehaving tourists.

The rooms may be revealed realistically (and expensively) on a revolving stage, or by one area behind a scrim that is changed in darkness, *or by any imaginative use of the stage.*

AUTHOR'S NOTE

Discussing theatrical style is as frustrating as discussing
acting, because so much of both are ethereal—but
realization of a play's style on a stage is crucial and,
in my opinion, the director's chief task. Some plays fit
comfortably into traditional styles with which we're
generally familiar—the sitcom, the kitchen-sink drama,
the cinematic narrative, the theatrical musical.
STONEWALL JACKSON'S HOUSE doesn't.

I am a verbal writer, and while I relish the visual and
theatrical aspects of a production, still, first and last,
the merit of my work excites or bores on the basis of
what the characters say. As in all my plays, the
characters of S J H are very real and should be played
as such—but what they say is frequently not "realistic".
Rather, it is the verbalization of their innermost, usually
unspoken thoughts and feelings. It is often spoken
subtext. The characters believe passionately in
everything they're saying—but are often unaware
of its effect on others.

On the one hand, the play is silly; on the other, it
couldn't be more serious. How does a director stage
and how do actors play this seeming contradiction?
On the one hand, if the actors distance themselves from
the characters and smirk at them—or if the director
allows them to be too broad—the whole things becomes
a cartoon (and, not incidentally, won't be funny); on the
other, if they play it "realistically," without comic sense,
the production becomes deadly. The thin line that

separates these two approaches constitutes the style of this play.

As for the longer speeches (particularly in Act Two), filling every moment becomes the actor's task. "But s/he wouldn't say that!" is an unhelpful exercise here. S/he *does* say it. The actors have no time off in this play. Almost all are onstage all the time—and all have plenty to say. In the New York production, they were generally wrung out after each performance—exhilarated when it went well, grumpy when it didn't.

I strongly suggest the director discuss the politics of the play with the actors *before* casting them. Although I welcome disagreement and outrage (it's why I wrote it!), this reaction needs to come from the audience—not from the cast. Obviously, this is not to say the actors should agree with everything the play says, but unless there is some uniform appreciation of its points of view—or at least the points of view being aired—the rehearsal process is liable to devolve into political harangue—"I buy this idea, but I don't buy that one"—and the performances, which need to be so committed to the characters, may be undermined.

Finally, the few references to New York may be changed to suit the individual needs of the theater producing the play—particularly those dependent for ticket sales upon the approval of one cultural medium, such as *The New York Times*.

"Gentlemen. We have a new foreman. Welcome to the foundry of lies."

Lambert Leroux in PRAVDA
by David Hare & Howard Brenton

ACT ONE

(At rise: LAWANDA and the two couples stand in front of the Stonewall Jackson House kitchen, which is furnished with chopping tables, a stove, and other items mentioned in the dialogue.)

LAWANDA: Good morning and welcome to the house of General Thomas Jonathan "Stonewall" Jackson. My name is LaWanda Gayle, and I'm your docent, or guide, through the Stonewall Jackson House. Now Stonewall Jackson owned only one house in his entire life, and this is it. Stonewall Jackson lived in this house two and a half years, from 1859 to 1861 when he went away to fight the Civil War. During the Civil War he only returned home twice, but this house stayed in his family many years after he was killed at the historic battle of Chancellorsville in 1863. Okay. Stonewall Jackson bought this house for his second wife, Mary Anna Morrison, in 1858, whom he loved very greatly. Stonewall Jackson had moved here to Lexington, Virginia, in 1851 to take up a teaching assignment at the Virginia Military Institute, or V M I, as it is more popularly known as.
The first room we'd like to visit is the Stonewall Jackson kitchen. Now as we wander throughout the house, we would like to encourage you to take as many photographs as you want, but kindly don't touch anything and, please, no flash. Now here we have, first of all, some knives of the period and the kind of chopping table where Stonewall Jackson and Mary

Anna might have done some chopping. Now Stonewall Jackson had chronic indigestion and probably an ulcer. And so he drank the natural spring water from Rockbridge Island Springs, Hot Springs, and Warm Springs, all in this part of Virginia, outta this demijohn. *(Aside)* Boy, I wish I could keep my mind on this. This is my eighth tour today, and I got a toothache split your head open Sunday. *(To others)* Now even though Mary Anna didn't like domestic chores, Stonewall Jackson *did* like domestic chores, and it's on the record that one day Stonewall Jackson canned ninety-nine heads of cabbage in one afternoon. It's hard but interesting to picture Stonewall Jackson, such a ferocious general in wartime, canning ninety-nine heads of cabbage, but he did.

(BARNEY and DEL laugh pleasantly, surprised.)

JUNIOR: I never heard that....

LAWANDA: *(Aside)* I can't believe how full of hate I am. *(To others)* Over here we have a one-hundred-percent authentic item owned by Stonewall Jackson and his wife Mary Anna, and it is called a rotor ruffler. And this is how the peoples of the time put ruffles or you might say pleats in their collars. The rods in here was taken out, put into the fire to get red hot, then the collars of the time was made damp, the red hot rods was inserted back into the ruffler, the collar was placed under the ruffler rotor, and the rotor of the ruffler would implant the ruffles.

BARNEY: Huh!

LAWANDA: It was considered very modern for the time, and they enjoyed it thoroughly.

DEL: Victorians were so clever, weren't they, Barn!

JUNIOR: This really belonged to them?

LAWANDA: Yes, sir.

(JUNIOR *and* MAG *take several photos quickly.*)

JUNIOR: How's it installed?

LAWANDA: With a screw. Two screws.

JUNIOR: Oh. Are they authentic?

LAWANDA: Well, they're authentic screws—

JUNIOR: No, no, I mean are they original with the house?

LAWANDA: No, they was put in last week.

JUNIOR: Oh. Modren.

MAG: Junior hates things that are modren.

LAWANDA: Oh. Now let's see, what else.... *(Aside)*
I can't remember a thing, I'm so distracted. That's
why Calvin took off. And 'cause he say I'm so passive.
Can't concentrate, can't make no decisions. Where am
I? Oh, yeah, the pitcher! *(To others)* The pitcher on the
shelf is the pitcher Stonewall Jackson drank lemonade
and buttermilk from as a boy, so you can look at that.
Now before we move on to the next room, does anyone
got any questions?

JUNIOR: Did the stove belong to him?

LAWANDA: Okay. The wood-burning four-burner stove
is from the period, and it is exactly the kind of stove it is
believed Stonewall Jackson and Mary Anna had in his
house.

JUNIOR: In other words—fake. Not like the bedroom,
I hope!

MAG: That's what we really came to see—Stonewall
Jackson's bedroom.

JUNIOR: That's really one-hundred-percent authentic,
isn't it?

LAWANDA: Yes, sir, it is.

JUNIOR: But really the only thing that belonged to him in here is the rotor ruffler and the lemonade-buttermilk pitcher, izzat right?

LAWANDA: In this room that is correct, though there are several items in other rooms which belonged to them both. You mentioned the famous bedroom for one. Now there's a tour right behind me, so if you'd like to take some pictures, please go right ahead, and then we can move on to Stonewall Jackson's study.

JUNIOR: Oh, what the hell. Let's get some of this stuff, even if it isn't real.

(He and MAG *photograph wildly.)*

LAWANDA: *(Aside)* I never understand why peoples wants pictures of this place—we got professional ones outside in the gift shop. Do they show em off? Does their friends axe 'em, "Oh, please, can we see your pictures of the interior of the Stonewall Jackson House?" Does they stretch out in front of the fire and reminisce about all the good times they had in this house? *(To others)* 'Nuff light?

MAG: Oh, yes. We use A S A 400, kick it to a thousand.

(The Study reveals itself. En route:)

DEL: How did he get the name "Stonewall?"

LAWANDA: In 1861 at Manassas he was given orders to stop the enemy, and, even though the fire was heavy, his regiment stood so stock still, they was called a stone wall.

DEL: Oh, how interesting. Thank you.

BARNEY: He was killed by his own men, wasn't he?

LAWANDA: Yes, sir. He was returning to his troops from a meeting, and they shot him by mistake.

DEL: How awful for his family!

LAWANDA: Yes, ma'am. Stonewall and Mary Anna Jackson had only one child while he was alive, though he only saw her twice or so before he died.

DEL: Oh, how sad for them...

BARNEY: Was he pretty much thought to be a good general?

LAWANDA: Didn't lose a battle.

JUNIOR: Well, not quite—won ten, lost one. Kernstown, 1862, first battle of the Shenandoah Valley. But he whipped 'em everyplace else!

LAWANDA: *(Aside)* Uh-oh. Somebody here has read a book.

MAG: And though he was ferocious and bloodthirsty in war, he was the sweetest, most considerate husband—

JUNIOR: One of the great love stories of all time, isn't it, guide.

LAWANDA: Oh, yes, I'm surprised it hasn't been made into a H B O Special Projeck by now. *(Aside)* Both of them has read books. I hate that, when the tourist know more than the guide.

JUNIOR: I ain't sorry those H B Os ain't done a show about him. Hollywood always turns our heroes into buffoons. 'Cause, really, it's a pretty unanimous fact the Civil War would've been won by the South if he'd of stayed alive.

LAWANDA: *(Aside)* Just what I want to hear—that the Civil War would've been won by the South. What am I doin' here in this house? Put a handkerchief on my head and call me Aunt Jemima! The man owned slaves!

BARNEY: You mean if Stonewall Jackson had lived, we'd still have slavery?

JUNIOR: Ho, that'd be just the beginnin'!

MAG: I'll say!

BARNEY: Terrible thing, slavery. We're from Ohio, so we know.

DEL: Awful, awful.

LAWANDA: *(Aside)* Yeah, right. Ohio? Where is that 'zackly? *(Aside)* Okay. Now we are coming to the liberry. Okay. Now the one thing you got to remember is Stonewall Jackson and Mary Anna Jackson loved each other very much. This was one of the great love stories of all time.

JUNIOR: We just said that!

LAWANDA: *(Aside)* Nothing goes right for me. We had such a happy family till I was born. *(To others)* Now Stonewall Jackson prepared for his class at V M I every night. He often spent three to five hours a night working on his lectures right at this handsome secretary.

BARNEY: Goodness—three to five hours!

JUNIOR: He memorized them word for word. Taught physics and artillery tactics.

MAG: He memorized 'em by rote. If he ever forgot something in class, he'd have to start right all over at the beginning.

JUNIOR: Students didn't like him. He wasn't much of a teacher.

LAWANDA: *(Aside)* Damn, next they be telling me the color of his horse's eyeballs.

DEL: How tall was he?

LAWANDA: Stonewall Jackson was five feet, eleven inches tall.

MAG: Five-nine.

LAWANDA: Oh. Uh, according to our manual—

JUNIOR: Your manual? Ha, ha, your manual?

MAG: Your manual?

(JUNIOR and MAG break up)

JUNIOR: Oh, no. Current scholarship contradicts that. In addition to Mary Anna's letters, Naomi Burtin's scholarly work, *Random Measurements of Confederate Generals*, she says he was five-nine, and if he was five-eleven, he would have had to stoop over to write on that there secretary. That proves it.

LAWANDA: Not necessarily. That there secretary isn't authentic.

JUNIOR: It isn't?

MAG: Oh, no, not another fake!

LAWANDA: *(Aside)* That was dumb, LaWanda. You ain't supposed to volunteer that unless they *axe* you if it's authentic.

BARNEY: Slavery must have been really terrible. The crass inhun..nity! Goes against my grain so...

LAWANDA: *(Aside)* Oh, I don't know. Compared to taking a couple of rednecks through this house, it wasn't so bad. We was kept warm, they give us clothes, everybody sure 'nuff had a job...

JUNIOR: It wasn't that bad. They was taken care of.

LAWANDA: *(Aside)* Somehow, for me to say slavery wadn't so bad's one thing; when he does it, all *I* see is guys hanging from trees.

JUNIOR: Look, little lady, LaWanda, I don't mean to be rude, but this is pretty damn frustrating. My name is Junior Nuckolls, and my wife Mag and me—

MAG: Each year Junior and me has a special projeck in American history—

LAWANDA: Oh.

MAG: Last year we did "James A Garfield: Ambidexterous Classicist."

BARNEY: He was ambidexterous?

MAG: He could write Greek with one hand and Latin with the other—simultaneously! Sort of stood for his whole administration. Which by the way only lasted one year.

BARNEY: How interesting!

JUNIOR: Year 'fore that, it was James K Polk. Nobody remembers it, but he was sorta responsible for America bein' so big.

DEL: Polk?

MAG: "Our manifest destiny is to overspread and possess the whole of the continent which Providence has given us."

DEL: So that's when it started.

BARNEY: Polk...Polk. I sort of forget what he did.

JUNIOR: Poor Polk had two problems: first, he didn't have his own nickname. Had to settle for "Young Hickory" cause evvybody hoped he's gonna be like "Old Hickory," Andy Jackson, which never happened. Second, school kids always mix him up with Franklin Pierce. Damn, history can break your heart.

MAG: We spent the whole year reading up on Polk, then took the Greyhound to Pineville, South Carolina, where he was born. A log cabin, by the way, long before Abe Lincoln and his P R spinmeisters ever heard of one!

JUNIOR: '94, we was so short of cash had to stay home and do Oglethorpe of Georgia, which was pathetic. So this year we saved for our dream and it's him.

DEL: What a grand idea! How long have you been doing this?

JUNIOR: Oh, six, seven years.

MAG: It can be anyone, as long as it's American and as long as he ain't modren.

JUNIOR: Oh, no, no modren! None of that modren furniture, houses, none of that Nelson Rockefeller bidness—

LAWANDA: Are you teachers?

JUNIOR: Oh, no, I'm in the bait bidness.

BARNEY: The bait business? What's that?

JUNIOR: Bait. I sit by the water and sell bait— gubbets, mungos, special whippies, you know—

MAG: And I'm his wife.

JUNIOR: On the Alabama side of the Peasman River, between Focus and Grand Libbit, Alabama.

BARNEY: Oh.

JUNIOR: So we're expecting quite a bit. We've read everything about him.

BARNEY: Is there a great deal written about him?

MAG: Oh, hundreds of things! *I Rode With Stonewall, The Stonewall Brigade, Stonewall Jackson: One Tooth Too Many.*

JUNIOR: *Stonewall Jackson: The Last Few Minutes of the First Few Days*—

MAG: I'd say the best text for the general reader is Mary Cotton Brigoon's *Tiny Metal Objects of the Civil War.*

JUNIOR: Then there is *Stonewall Jackson: What He Ate*—

MAG: *His Hair and Why—*

LAWANDA: Wow! *(Aside)* They's scary. We only get a twenty-five-page manual for this whole house; not like Colonial Williamsburg, where they get two hundred pages for each *room*. My tooth is killing me!

JUNIOR: Did you know he said, "You may be whatever you resolve to be?"

LAWANDA: Yes, sir, that's the first thing they teach us here.

JUNIOR: Well, at least they taught you something, guide!

LAWANDA: *(Aside)* This is what I left Richmond for? Hate that big city. Thought I'd like a small town where there's no competition—'steada all them politics 'bout how everybody hates us. But this ain't no better. And now I got some kind of skinhead *Jeopardy* champs on my tour.

BARNEY: Are you all right, LaWanda?

LAWANDA: *(Snapping out of it)* Oh, uh, yes, Mr—

BARNEY: Goshen. But please call me Barney. This is my first wife Del, and we're on our way to Monticello. I think you're doing a splendid job.

LAWANDA: Yeah?

BARNEY: We live in Granville, Ohio, a small university town filled with white, high-steepled churches, students in varsity sweaters and sorority pins, much quiet jogging on the footpaths....

DEL: It's a comfortable life; we're not ambitious, but we worked hard and made a lot of money anyway. Always wanted a son or a daughter.

BARNEY: A daughter, really. Sons, we feel, are mean.

DEL: We own a six-hundred-acre farm in Granville,
tilled by sturdy toilers. Barney sells insurance on the
phone.

BARNEY: And Del's one of the town librarians. Monday,
Thursday, and Saturday, eleven to three. It not only
stimulates her, it's good for the community.

DEL: Our feet are almost the same size.

BARNEY: Sweat gathers slowly but meaningfully for Del
and me. Summers we go for vacations together. We
always talk in low tones to each other. I smooth her hair.

DEL: I rub his hand.

BARNEY: In Granville, the grass is green and spiky
in the summer, the snow clean and thick in winter;
we treat the people who work for us very well.

DEL: They're entitled; they have our respect, our
loyalty. Once they're there, they never leave us.

LAWANDA: Gee, that sounds nice. (Aside) Spiky grass
and thick, clean snow, the honest work of a farm.
I never knew a life like that. Never knew anyone who
had a life like that. I never knew anyone who knew a
cousin who'd had a life like that.

JUNIOR: You folks really got it cushy, don't you...

BARNEY: We've been very fortunate, as I'm sure you
have been in the bait business.

MAG: (Disgusted) The bait bidness... Stinking hands—

JUNIOR: —two fires with no insurance—

MAG: —hot, long hours, Peasman's all toxic—

JUNIOR: —gummint's all over us dawn to dark. And for
what?

MAG: Dollar bills! That's what we live for. Sweaty little
dollar bills.

BARNEY: Come visit us up North. We'll make you feel right at home. Go for long walks, rake and burn leaves in the fall; most of my friends smoke a pipe.

LAWANDA: *(Aside)* That sounds so...seductive.
So trouble-free...

JUNIOR: Who can afford to go to Ohio? Whole year's allowance out the window comin' to this clip joint.

MAG: I mean, six hundred miles plus gas and so far outta two rooms we got a thing that makes ruffles in collars, a buttermilk pitcher, and a housefula fakes, that right?

LAWANDA: Oh, uh, well, technically, yes'm, but—

JUNIOR: "Yes, but technically?" Don't you give her no "Yes, but technically!"

LAWANDA: Well now, sir, but wait till you see what's next. Here is the parlor, where Stonewall Jackson used to teach Sunday school class every week to the colored children. He was very devoted to the little children and was an elder in the Presbyterian Church. *(Aside)* What am I gonna do with these snarlin' hillbillies? Now I got a *headache* and a toothache. *(To others)* Okay. In this room, Stonewall Jackson and Mary Anna would spend their evenings after he finished preparing his lectures. He'd read to her every night, 'cause he knew the candlelight would hurt her eyes.

JUNIOR: These books his?

LAWANDA: All Stonewall Jackson's books is in the Museum of the Confederacy in Richmond.

JUNIOR: I can't stand it! I'm gonna go faint like a woman! Ain't nothing authentic in the whole place!

LAWANDA: No, you in for a happy surprise, Mr Nuckolls. Set your gaze on this horsehair sofa. It is one-hundred-percent authentic.

JUNIOR: It is?

MAG: Oh, thank God!

(*They prepare to photograph it.* LAWANDA *moves between them and the couch*)

LAWANDA: However, I am sorry to report, Mr Nuckolls, that that sofa is the one object in the house you're not allowed to photograph.

JUNIOR: What! Why not!

MAG: What kind of a shyster hell-hole is this!

LAWANDA: The light waves absorbed by your camera's lens could do irreparable damage to the upholstery.

JUNIOR: What!

MAG: The light waves?

LAWANDA: *(Aside)* This is a lie. This is such a lie, and it feels so good. *(To others)* I'm sorry, sir, that is not my decision, it is the policy of the United States Government and the Commonwealth of Virginia, which owns and operates us.

JUNIOR: But I've photographed things much older'n this sofa! Much!

MAG: James K Polk's stuff was all older!

LAWANDA: It's not my fault, sir. But I will have to confiscate you and your wife's cameras if you don't quit takin' pictures.

JUNIOR: What?!

LAWANDA: *(Aside)* I'ze in heaven.

JUNIOR: You think this is some cheap disposable? You lay one hand on this camera, and I'll—

MAG: You know somethin', sister? I never heard of no policy about light waves hurtin' no furniture, and me and Junior've had just about enougha you and this devil-ugly house!

BARNEY: Now just a moment. Junior, Mag, these rules aren't LaWanda's fault. And I happen to think this house is beautiful.

JUNIOR: Well, you're wrong!

MAG: Beautiful? I've seen compost prettiern this!

BARNEY: *(Soothingly)* Sometimes we have disputes on the farm in Ohio. I take the men out among the sheep. We talk things out in low, rumbling *timbres* that can't be overheard. There's something soothing about a flock of sheep—especially if they're not jumping.

DEL: They have a glass of spring water right at the spring—just as Stonewall may have done here.

BARNEY: We always come back revived and heartened.

LAWANDA: Sounds like paradise...

JUNIOR: Oh, no you don't. You're going to be looking for a new job by the time my dear Mag here gets my supper on the table! A new job without no kind of gummint quota crutch!

LAWANDA: *(Aside)* How am I supposed to deal with those two—I can't get no new job! Should I tell him he can photograph the sofa? *(The lights go out around LAWANDA. She is in a pin spot.)* My whole life's been like this. Abandoned by my father and mother at three, raised by a blind sister with diabetes; an early smoker and crackhead; flunk out the tenth grade. They had to scrape me up off the sidewalk in Richmond one morning after I been beat up by some pissed-off tricks. I got every V D you can think of. Only reason I ain't in jail now is cause of a judge couldn't keep his eyes offa my butt. No direction, no purpose—didn't got no goal then, don't got one now. And now this: a toothache through my brain and a nasty bait salesman from Alabama just waiting for Lurleen Wallace to come back from the dead. Last night I got my sixteenth parking ticket, and in June some gangstas killed my dog. Oh, and I'm being audited by the U S Government! Me! Only twenty-three and I'm being audited! What's next? I couldn't get into no schools with two times affirmative action; no friends, no job, no future. Who's ever looked out for me but me?

(Lights fade on LAWANDA, *come up on a beautiful dining room. It is 1861.* BARNEY, *dressed in the handsome gray and gold uniform of the Confederacy, sits at the table eating partridge with* DEL, *who is dressed in luxurious red velvet. Without missing a beat, serves them dinner.)*

BARNEY: My dear, it looks as though Joe Johnston and Sam Hood's got 'em on the run! And Stonewall at Manassas! And Harper's Ferry—we captured twelve thousand Yankees! If we can just lick 'em at Fredericksburg, I think we may be able to preserve this emerald land free and independent forever.

DEL: That's wonderful news, Mr Goshen. A short war would benefit us all.

BARNEY: Yes, indeed. What else is for supper, LaWanda? That partridge was mighty tasty, wasn't it Mrs Goshen?

DEL: Mighty, Mr Goshen.

LAWANDA: We got the lubbol, halves of chicken with the dowdy, parboiled muffins, liver pudding, sausage and apple toddy with molasses....

BARNEY: Ahh, delicious. But then you and Calvin always feed us so well.

LAWANDA: Thank you, Marse Goshen.

DEL: How are the chirren? Claiborne? Little Ninna? How is Little Ninna?

LAWANDA: Claiborne's Cole's all better, and Little Ninna, her infections healed straight up. What you did work puffick.

DEL: Bless your heart. What about yo' eight other chirren?

LAWANDA: They's fine, maam.

BARNEY: You look as though something's botherin' you, LaWanda.

LAWANDA: Oh, it's just a little toothache. It don't matter....

DEL: *(Getting up)* Let me have a look.

(She forces LAWANDA over the table and examines her)

LAWANDA: Oh no, missis, it's not important, not during yo' supper—

DEL: This is more important than our old supper, good as it is. Now open up—I see it. This won't take a second.

LAWANDA: No, no, missis, I got to get the lollop fuh you—Aaaahhhh!

(DEL pulls her tooth dramatically.)

DEL: There—got it. Here, bite down on this.

LAWANDA: Gee, that didn't hurt a bit! It feels better already. You surely does take care of us, Marse Goshen, Miz Goshen—clothes, shelter, taxes, nussin', da Bible—

BARNEY: Well, you're family, LaWanda. We love you. And y'all work so hard for us.

DEL: We're a team. Your life is our life.

LaWanda: You even name our chirrun for us sometimes. I bet them Yankees don't look atter they own families good as you do atter mine.

Barney: I don't know about their own families, but they surely do 'spise us.

LaWanda: Excuse me, suh, Marse Goshen, but if the Yankee hates us so much, how come he so hongry to hold onto us?

Barney: They made a fortune importing and selling slaves, but now that there's no profit in it, they get all righteous and demand that we—whom they took the profits *from*—gotta give 'em up. For free!

Del: Envy and meddlin' started this war—not this sanctimonious emancipation flag they wrap themselves in.

Barney: Tell you what, let the Yankees reimburse us what we paid them, I'll be glad to free every one! 'Course you know you and Calvin and your ten children can be free anytime you want....

LaWanda: No suh! You be good to us, take care of us...what would we do? Where'd we go?

Barney: Why up North, do whatever Nigras do up North. Be free!

LaWanda: (*Frightened*) Don't you talk like that, Marse Goshen! No, sir! We don't want to free! You too good to us. You ain't thinkin' about doin' that, is you?

Del: No, LaWanda, we're not thinking about doing that, not if you don't want it.

Barney: You tell Calvin not to worry about a thing. We'll take care of all of you.

(*Lights go down on the supping Goshens, pin spot up on* LaWanda.)

LAWANDA: *(Aside)* All cream and sugar on the outside, maybe. *Then* they beat you. Be a fool to live like that. I be just as passive as I is now. "Yassa, nossa," jump when they sneeze. I don't make no difference now, didn't make no difference then. Nobody need me now, nobody need me then. Or did they?

(Lights come up on BARNEY, *now in a torn and filthy Confederate uniform, and* DEL, *her burgundy velvet dress in tatters. It is 1865. They are exhausted from years of fighting.)*

BARNEY: They burned Miz Holcomb's to the ground!

DEL: If only they'd leave us the cotton—so we could get back on our feet, have a chance at least.

BARNEY: Never thought this war would go on for four years. Sherman wasn't as bad as this new man Potter. Sherman just took the horses.

DEL: Ever since Stonewall was cut down at Chancellorsville, we've been a ship of state without a rudder. He was so strong, gave us such hope. The whole Confederacy seemed cut down with him.

*(*LAWANDA *rushes in with a baby.)*

LAWANDA: Marse Goshen, Miz Goshen, they right at the gate! Hurry, massa, hurry—they kill you or take you prisoner! Into the cellar!

BARNEY: No, LaWanda, this is my home, my land—

LAWANDA: You ain't got no time to be prideful! I won't let them downstairs! Go, go!

(In the background flames glow. LAWANDA *gives* DEL *her baby.)*

LAWANDA: An' you, ma'am, take my baby Hippolyte. Maybe they won't bother you if you got a baby. Just don't let them see she's colored. Here!

DEL: Where's Calvin?

LAWANDA: I sent him downstairs with the babies and the silver. If they see him, they be enlistin' him in the Yankee army!

BARNEY: I'm not budging!

LAWANDA: Then you let LaWanda bandage your leg, Marse Goshen. Maybe the Yankees ain't so low, they let a wounded man alone. I use the sugarbeet for blood. *(She bandages* BARNEY's *leg)* Now you limp, Marse Goshen, you limp fo' yo' life!

(There is much racket. The flames glow redder in the background. JUNIOR *enters, dressed as a mangy Union officer. He carries a half-eaten mutton chop in his hand; his mouth is smeared with mutton grease.)*

JUNIOR: Well, look what we have here! Caught you red-handed. *(Yelling offstage)* Shoot all the animals— I want all of 'em dead, just like the place across the river! *(To others)* All right, where's your silver? *(No answer)* Hey, you know who we are? We are Potter's Raid! Already burned your cotton—

DEL: Oh no!

JUNIOR: —already set fire to your stables and all the outbuildings, took your horses, butchered your animals—

LAWANDA: Oh no, sir, no, sir—

JUNIOR: And we're gonna burn this pretty building here to the ground—

DEL: No!

JUNIOR: —unless you tell us where your silver is!

DEL: But that's everything we've got! You've burned all the rest! We'll never get back on our feet....

JUNIOR: Why should you? You lost. They lost, didn't they, mammy?

LaWANDA: Yes suh.

JUNIOR: Well now, you're free and all, you comin' with us?

LaWANDA: No suh.

JUNIOR: Going up North with family and friends?

LaWANDA: No suh.

JUNIOR: Well, whatta ya gonna do?

LaWANDA: I stays here.

JUNIOR: Stays here? With them? But you've missed the point of the whole war! Don't you know? They treat you like trash! Beat you, abuse you, rape you!

LaWANDA: Only ones done that was the Yankees comin' through.

JUNIOR: What! Oh you're one of the bad darkies. I heard about Negroes like you—just bad through and through. Well, I don't care what you do—none of you will have a place to live when I'm through with you. Now where's the silver!

(No answer)

(JUNIOR smacks BARNEY in the leg with his sword. BARNEY shrieks and falls to the floor.)

BARNEY: Ohhhhh! My leg! *(JUNIOR whacks him once more. DEL faints; LaWANDA picks up the crying baby.)*

LaWANDA: Stop this, Mr Yankee man! Is all of 'em up there like you? Beat an ole man got nothin' left outta his life, make a woman faint with a babe in her arms, and she already two months carrying? !

JUNIOR: She's gonna have a baby? But she's fifty-five!

LaWANDA: Is you what all Yankees is like? Kill animals, burn crops, whup people who ain't had

nothin' to eat in four days? Kill women and unborn
chirrun? Is all Yankees without honor?

JUNIOR: Well, no, I didn't mean to—

LAWANDA: An' here we waited so long for you to come
liberate us and treat us like humans, and this is what's
meant by Yankee justice? Scold, scold on you,
Massachusetts shame!

(He holds his head low.)

JUNIOR: I am a shame. And a disgrace! We'll let you be.
(Calling) Men! Put out those fires! Leave that cotton
alone! You really ain't had nothing to eat for four days?

(She nods. He hands her the greasy mutton chop.)

JUNIOR: Here. *(Calling)* Morosini! Carvalho! Put
everything back! Tie up those drapes! I want this place
like new when we leave! You know what I've always
said: "Leave the interior space looking better than when
you found it for the sake of the next fellow!"

*(He exits. They wait until he's fully gone, then jump up and
embrace each other.)*

LAWANDA: He's gone!

DEL: Oh, LaWanda, LaWanda! You saved our lives,
our home!

BARNEY: We owe you everything!

LAWANDA: Hush now, Marse Goshen! What you think
family is for? *(They hug and laugh. Lights back up on the
tour.* JUNIOR *is changed back into his contemporary clothes;*
BARNEY *and* DEL *change in front of the audience.)*

JUNIOR: Know what I think? I think this is just a greedy
gummint trap for innocent out-of-state tourists!

LAWANDA: *(Aside)* My toothache's gone....

JUNIOR: I ain't lettin' you get away with this, guide!

LAWANDA: *(Aside)* I know what I have to do now.

MAG: And if you're an example of a guide, I'd ruther buy a book!

LAWANDA: *(Aside)* It's so clear, so shimmering. Why didn't I come to this before? I did make a difference! History will teach us everything.

JUNIOR: Come all the way up from 'Bama for this? Get by the frost, get by the drought, pay off the inspector, and for what, guide?

LAWANDA: *(Aside)* I want to sip cold water from a spring like Stonewall, pound the bread with purpose, roll around in the snow, dance naked on the spiky summer grass, sing till my bosom burst from joy....

JUNIOR: Are you listening to us? Are you?

LAWANDA: *(Aside)* Because underneath this confused and battered exterior beats the heart of a swooning romantic. So it's either kill myself or...or.... *(To others)* Mr Goshen, Mrs Goshen, do you have any openings on your farm?

BARNEY: *(Surprised)* What? Well, we do have openings from time to time....

LAWANDA: Could I fill one?

BARNEY: Fill one? As what exactly, LaWanda?

LAWANDA: I want to be your slave.

JUNIOR: Huh?

LAWANDA: I want to go with you and work your farm.

JUNIOR: Maybe you ain't so bad after all.

LAWANDA: I'm a good housekeeper, I can cook, serve you dinner, I can even work the fields—it's in m'blood!

DEL: Well, we could certainly quite possibly employ you, yes, but—

LAWANDA: No Ma'am, thank you, but I'm not talking
about employment, I'm talking about slavery—uncruel
but abject. You can't beat me or be mean to me, but
aside from that I want to be your property. My whole
life is some kind of permanent bone cancer, and I got to
get out of it else I'm gonna die—today. I'll work hard
for you, ma'am, hard as you want. And in return you
handle my money, decide what I want to do in life,
do my concentrating fuh me, get me to a doctor when
I needs it, figure out which sexuality I like, pick out my
clothes and friends, and bury me when it's over. I don't
ever want to figger out taxes or parking tickets, hafta
choose a H M O, keep track of no frequent flyer miles,
go to school, hunt down no jobs, or decide if Jesse
Jackson's right or not. And mainly what I don't want
most is to make any more decisions after this one!
You own me—the lock, the stock, and the barrel.

BARNEY: Is your life really that bad, LaWanda?

LAWANDA: Yup.

DEL: But all those things are part of the growing-up
process. You'll get over it.

LAWANDA: Growing up is knowing what you want
and going after it. I want to be your slave, and I'm
going after slavery. I won't get over it.

JUNIOR: But what if they beat you, treat you bad,
whup you like in the old days?

LAWANDA: I thought you said they never did that.

JUNIOR: They didn't! Well, not unless someone
deserved it. What if you deserved it?

BARNEY: Mr Nuckolls, how dare you!

DEL: My God, you're a dark rascal!

JUNIOR: Yeah, yeah, but well...?

LAWANDA: They won't beat me or treat me bad.
I can tell by their eyes.

BARNEY: *(Red in the face)* May my hands be cut off if
ever I raise one finger 'gainst this girl!

DEL: *(Angry, too)* Is that clear, Mr Nuckolls?

JUNIOR: Yeah, yeah, I was just asking.

LAWANDA: Please, Mr Goshen!

JUNIOR: You really want to be a...a slave?

LAWANDA: Yes, sir!

JUNIOR: Well, come be our slave! Come dig up worms
in the mud for us.

MAG: What a dream...our own property! Just like we
was promised!

LAWANDA: Uh...no thank you, sir. Mr Goshen—?

BARNEY: Well, I don't know....

DEL: We'll have to talk it over, LaWanda.

(They confer upstage.)

JUNIOR: What do you mean, "No thank you, sir?"
How come you'll slave it up for them but not for us?

MAG: We not good enough for you? Why, you uppity—

LAWANDA: Mr Goshen, please hurry!

JUNIOR: Maybe we just oughtta take you out back—

BARNEY: All right! We'll do it. We'll be responsible for
your life.

LAWANDA: Oh, thank you, Mr Goshen!

JUNIOR: What? You actually gonna let her be your slave?

DEL: That's what she wants. And that's what we want.

BARNEY: Of course, we're not going to call you slave...

DEL: What if we called you an "associate"?

LAWANDA: Nope. Slave.

JUNIOR: Actually, we didn't call 'em slaves. We called 'em servants.

BARNEY: Well, what if we called you a servant?

LAWANDA: Well...all right!

(They cheer and embrace. JUNIOR and MAG are thoroughly disgusted.)

JUNIOR: I never seed such stuff.

MAG: Very trashy personnel.

BARNEY: When would you like to start?

LAWANDA: Right away. But first I want to show Mag and Junior here that this house ain't no rip-off. We have yet to see Stonewall Jackson's famous bedroom. In that room, everything's authentic.

MAG: Oh my God, I almost forgot!

JUNIOR: Hurry up, guide, hurry up.

LAWANDA: The bed is an authentic canopied four poster, with Victorian ropes instead of springs, all the spreads and pillows, the dresser, his shaving bowl, commode, razor, and strop are authentic, the entire room a hymn to Victoriana!

JUNIOR: This is more than I ever thought! Dreamed!

MAG: I can't wait—my knees are trembling!

LAWANDA: Voilà!

(The Stonewall Jackson bedroom reveals itself. There is not a Victorian piece in it. It's all modern. In the center is the modernist bed Nelson Rockefeller donated to the United States when he was Vice President. JUNIOR and MAG are stunned.)

mag + Junior are miserable

JUNIOR: That ain't his bed!

MAG: That ain't his room!

JUNIOR: That didn't belong to Stonewall Jackson!

MAG: Never!

JUNIOR: Didn't belong to Stonewall Jackson, Andy Jackson, or Reggie Jackson!

MAG: That's Nelson and Happy Rockefeller's bed!

JUNIOR: What! Lied to again! Where's my ax?

MAG: We been clowned out again! This is all Bauhaus!

JUNIOR: Gropius chairs, Breuer tables, Corbusier chaise!

LAWANDA: How did this happen?

BARNEY: You mean it doesn't usually look like this?

LAWANDA: No sir! Usually Stonewall Jackson's bedroom!

JUNIOR: *(Falling to his knees and crying)* Why does this always happen to us? So much torture, so much despair!

MAG: *(Crying too)* We plan, we work, we scrimp and save, everything goes wrong!

LAWANDA: *(Kindly)* Is it just bad luck, maybe?

JUNIOR: Sometimes luck, sometimes we just ruin it ourselves.

MAG: Peoples always against us—gummints send lawyers, our friends don't like us—

JUNIOR: We walk down a street, people get mad just lookin' at us!

MAG: We can't get anything to work!

JUNIOR: Couldn't even have chirrun! I'm sterile, she's barren.

Barney offers to take them in. 27

MAG: Ain't easy bein' white trash.

JUNIOR: If I didn't have her, I'd be dead by now.

MAG: If I didn't have him, *I'd* be dead by now.

JUNIOR: This century's too hard, God! First kudzu, now this furniture—!

BARNEY: Come live with us.

JUNIOR: What?

BARNEY: We'll take care of you.

DEL: We'll lift care from your shoulders like a cloak.

BARNEY: You'll feel as if you're floating....

JUNIOR: You mean...like her?

DEL: Yes.

MAG: Be slaves?

BARNEY: You'll have to work—but we'll take care of everything else. Come and enjoy the rolling hills.

DEL: Summers in Granville are humid, but our spring water salves and cools.

JUNIOR: You mean...slave it up with her?

DEL: Well, you *will* have to work that out. But it shouldn't be so hard. Your needs are the same.

JUNIOR: I haven't seen a lamb since 1972!

BARNEY: We'll wait outside.

(BARNEY, DEL, *and* LAWANDA *exit.*)

JUNIOR: God, sounds like heaven, don't it?

MAG: Like heaven...celestial cherubim and everythin'...

JUNIOR: What do you say, sugarbus?

MAG: Whatever you say, Junior. I'd like to....

JUNIOR: So would I.

(They kiss.)

MAG: I love you, Junior.

JUNIOR: And I love you, sugarbus.

JUNIOR & MAG: We're coming, Stonewall!

(They exit, music swells as in the ending of a play, lights dim…)

(…and pop back up on a Rehearsal Room in midtown Manhattan. OZ, TRACY, GABY, *and* CLAIRE *are in shock over the play they've just seen.)*

OZ: Lights!

TRACY: Jesus!

GABY: God!

OZ: Now, now—

TRACY: *(Angrily)* Who funded this?

GABY: It is infuriating!

TRACY: What a waste of a workshop!

GABY: It's absurd, just absurd—

CLAIRE: But not Absurdist—

GABY: Why on earth did you approve this, Tracy? Why is it even under consideration?

TRACY: Oz never let me read it.

OZ: Now, that's not exactly true—

GABY: This is the play you've been talking about for three weeks? Why on earth did you want to direct *this*?

CLAIRE: *(Looking at a script) Stonewall Jackson's House* by Joe Rock.

GABY: Just how many grants do you want us to lose?

OZ: Now, Gaby—

GABY: It's a goddam sitcom!

OZ: It is not a sitcom—

TRACY: It sure as hell is not a sitcom!

OZ: I think the guy's a good writer, and we're here to help writers.

GABY: My God, this is supposed to be the theater, man!

OZ: Come on, give it a chance, will you? I think what we have here is a very imaginative play, gutsy, very theatrical, with a great deal to say—

TRACY: I'm so mad I can't sit down!

GABY: Really, Oz, let's just move on to the next one.

TRACY: Ho no. I want the son-of-a-bitch who wrote this downstage center—preferably at the end of a rope!

OZ: That's not how we do things, you know that, Gaby. *(Shouting into audience)* Joe!

GABY: In the theater you need to be moved, shaken, enriched and ennobled—

JOE: *(O S) (Surly)* Yes!

GABY: —have the eyes forced open with tent pegs if necessary!

OZ: *(To JOE)* Would you come in, please?

JOE: *(O S)* No!

OZ: *(To JOE)* But it's your play!

JOE: *(O S)* Nope!

GABY: I don't blame him. You always go off on tangents like this, Oz. Two or three hits, then you get *avant-garde.*

OZ: Well, I'm not backing down on this one, Gabriella.

Kaplan Macklow Theatre

GABY: That's what you said about all those Irish plays. Remember when you wanted to do an entire season of Irish plays?

OZ: Well, the one we did do won an Obie.

GABY: *One* Obie.

OZ: *(To* JOE*)* Now, Joe, we want you to have your say. Constructive criticism is the foundation of the Kaplan Macklow Theater. Don't you want your play in the Festival?

JOE: *(O S)* But they hate it!

OZ: No, they don't! Now, Joe, we're not here to rewrite your play. Such may be the ways of fascist government, but that's not our way at the Macklow. We respect each playwright for the singular voice with which she or he has been gifted. Kap Macklow was a very great critic, which is why we named the theater after him, and if he were alive today, he would applaud your play, because it epitomizes what we call our Vision 2000 Program—

GABY: 2010.

OZ: We agreed on Vision 2000.

GABY: But what happens in 2001? We'll be behind the curve again!

OZ: But Vision 2010 sounds so clumsy. Look, could we leave this for the board meeting, dear? *(Back to* JOE*)* You see, in order to bring the Macklow into the Twenty-first Century, we are committed to making over seventy-five percent of our productions nontraditional. People of color, women, the sexually precarious—

TRACY: Plays of controversy—

OZ: We certainly don't shy from controversy—

JOE: *(O S)* I know all this shit!

CLAIRE: Seventy-five percent?

OZ: Long been a dream of Gaby's and mine, Claire.

TRACY: A two-million-dollar grant kicks in if we do.

CLAIRE: Ahhh.

JOE: I'm not coming up there!

OZ: Well, we'll begin without you, then.

(Seating GABY)

OZ: You had some problems with *Stonewall Jackson's House*, didn't you, Gabriella?

GABY: Some problems? That's like saying I had "some problems" with my chemo. It's an appalling, distasteful little comic book, littered with characters who are just pure—very pure—one-and-a-half dimensional. And so mean-spirited. You have a highly developed spleen, young man.

OZ: Sometimes people *are* mean-spirited.

GABY: Well, they shouldn't be. Strindberg would be produced every day if he weren't so mean-spirited. You don't really want to put this on in the Festival, Oz—

OZ: Well, I think we should at least discuss it, Gaby. Just because there's nothing for you to play in it—

GABY: There's nothing for anybody to play in it! The characters are all one-and-a-half-dimensional cartoons! I could play any or all of them if I wanted to, but I wouldn't go near them with...with a barge pole! *(To JOE)* What you should do, young man, is go check out *Nothing Is Anybody's Fault* or *The Crucible*. Those are plays!

OZ: But the playwright has to have his own process. You do the same thing to me at home all the time! We've only got two hours, and we have four more one-acts to see.

MS mag 32 (girl) racist!

GABY: All right, if you want to wear your Mr Trains-Run-On-Time chapeau, why did you want to direct it?

OZ: Well...it's bold, original, and, most important, speaks to our time. Here you've got a complex setup with a young girl who—

GABY: Bitch! Slut!

OZ: What?

GABY: I can't stand it, *Ms* magazine has been published for thirty years, and you're still calling them "girls!" Why don't you just call them bitches and sluts?

OZ: Are you questioning my politics after all these years? Yes, all right, the play's about this young *woman*, who's obviously unhappy, who's being taken advantage of—

TRACY: Goddammit, can't any of you see it? THIS PLAY IS RACIST!!

(There is a moment of silence. Everyone is uncomfortable.)

OZ: Yes, well, we discussed that.

GABY: *(Just occurred to her)* That's right—racist, too!

TRACY: A black woman who chooses to go into slavery? What do you think we were watching up there?

OZ: Now, wait a second, Tracy, you can't just jump to conclusions like that—

TRACY: Are you black?

OZ: That's not the point—

TRACY: Are you black?

OZ: Tracy—

TRACY: You're not black, you never will be, and you have no conception of what it means to *be* black.

OZ: Of course I can't ever know *exactly* what it means to be black, but that doesn't mean I can't tell whether a play's racist or not.

GABY: I am a Jew. (*This stops everything.*)

OZ: We know that, dear. Why is that important now?

GABY: Because when a play's anti-Semitic I know it right through to my bones—much more than anyone would who's not a Jew. And I'm offended by this play.

OZ: Jesus, Gabriella. The one thing the play's not is anti-Semitic—

GABY: It would be if it were about a Jew.

OZ: But it's not about a Jew! It's about a young black girl—

GABY: Bitch! Slut!

OZ: —a young black *woman*, who's miserable, and everybody's picking on her, she's led a miserable life—

GABY: No African-American woman in today's South is going to dress up like a mammy to work in the house of a Confederate general, would she, Tracy!

TRACY: Well—

GABY: I mean, if the play's entire premise is unbelievable, how can the dramatic events which unfold thereafter be remotely plausible?

OZ: (*After a pause*) Well, aside from the racism, how'd you like it?

TRACY: There *is* nothing aside from the racism!

OZ: Now, Tracy, don't be dogmatic. Surely if you were in front of your undergrads you'd explore your distaste in greater depth.

TRACY: (*Suppressing her anger*) All right. A, you don't like any of the characters. B, in terms of literary value, the, uh, the desperate attempts at stylization are derivative; they numb. False, neo-Stoppardian wordplay (in itself and by definition sub-Nabokovian) bewilders, leaving the spectator anxious for the genuine article. The author confuses, with an arbitrarily Pinter-black segue here, a Beckett-bleak silence there. Provocative? I'll say. Stimulating? Harumph. But the middle of the play becomes overtly Ortonian, one is tempted to say even Fo-like. Where is the Mametian, the Shepardite, even the Fugarditic? And the supposedly satiric scholastical parodies—i e, the riff on Stonewalliana—while aspiring to a Shavian astringency, fail to reach either the Wassersteinian, the Kushnerite, or even an acute Guareness. And, in an effort to limn contemporary *angst* by employing a quasi-Sartrerian, hopelessly post-Brechtical style, the fledgling scribe reveals merely an unpleasant, Connecticut-inspired looking down his nose at the characters which can only be described as a Cheeverian *snarl* coupled with a Judeo-Protestant patriarchal *smile* in what I like to call a postmodern, semideconstructionist, pseudopainterly Sondheimeronianesque *snile*. How's that?

GABY: Who are all these people?

TRACY: And God knows the ending is unearned.

GABY: This has touched a nerve in Tracy few of us will ever fully appreciate. Let's go straight to the surgery: it's not a play! It isn't theater! It wasn't moving, there was no ennoblement, no enrichment, not a shred of dignity!

OZ: Oh, there was plenty of dignity. More important, it makes a profound statement for our time—

TRACY: Which is what?

OZ: Well, in my view, the play is about the need for a welfare state.

GABY: A welfare state? Ha ha! A welfare state?

OZ: Yes—some people need to be taken care of.
That's what the play's saying.

TRACY: No, it isn't!

GABY: There's no one to sympathize with, young man,
who are we supposed to root for?

OZ: This isn't the movies, Gaby. You don't have to
"root for" somebody.

GABY: It doesn't make any difference if it's the movies
or the living, breathing theater—you've got to root for
somebody.

JOE: (O S) Who do you "root for" in Oedipus at Colonus?

GABY: What?

OZ: And I happen to think LaWanda is very
sympathetic. I feel sorry for her, I want her to
change her life.

GABY: You feel sorry for her, Oz, or contempt? Isn't she
really just a cliché—though, admittedly, she's the first
African-American crackhead I've ever seen on a stage
with Attention Deficit Disorder. This is just fodder for
the cannons of the fascist Right. No one like her exists,
and it's racist and irresponsible of this author to put her
on a stage!

(JOE storms onstage from the house, crosses to each of them
threateningly)

JOE: Who are you people? What are you doing to me?
I give you my passion, my brain, my guts, everything
I have, forge it white hot on the anvil of my art, and
you crucify me, crucify me!

CLAIRE: This must be the writer.

GABY: (To CLAIRE) I like them better when they're
self-deprecating, don't you?

JOE: What gives you the right to trash my life to bits with your big black boots?

OZ: Now Joe, settle down. We were talking about your play—

JOE: Oh, yes, my play, my beautiful, poetic, racist play! The characters are unrealistic, situations unbelievable, and nobody black'd ever take a job like that, am I right so far? Well, do you want to know *how* I came to write this racist play? I was *in* Stonewall Jackson's House in Lexington, Virginia, where the tour guide *was* black and twenty-three, dressed *exactly* like I wrote, with a pitiful memorized spiel which I went back a second and a third time with a tape recorder to make sure I got right, who *hated* what she was doing, who kept losing her train of thought, who was bullied by a couple of sinister hicks from Georgia who knew a lot more about Stonewall Jackson than she did, and all I could see on her face was misery and despair and the desire to dig a hole, crawl into it, and die!

GABY: You mean everything in this play actually happened?

JOE: No, no of course not!

GABY: Because just because something really happens doesn't make it art.

JOE: I know that! You can't knife me from both sides! She and lots of others like her do exist, and I know that doesn't make it art, *I* make it art!

CLAIRE: Or not.

JOE: *(This stops him.)* What's your name again?

CLAIRE: Claire.

JOE: Okay, Claire, how can it be racist—both LaWanda *and* the rednecks, as you call them, go into slavery.

GABY: So?

slavery = racial welfare?
some people must be taken care of.

JOE: So, the rednecks are white! How can it be racist if both races do the same thing? And for the same reason?

TRACY: Which is what?

JOE: They both hate their lives and want to be taken care of! It has nothing to do with race! It's just what Oz said—some people need to be taken care of.

CLAIRE: Oh, a closet liberal.

OZ: Yes, you see, the couple from Ohio represents the state, and everybody else're the people who need help.

JOE: Yes! He can see it, why can't the rest of you?

TRACY: That's ridiculous!

CLAIRE: She does go into slavery, Oz...

JOE: But not Nineteenth Century slavery! LaWanda says, "You can't beat me, you can't treat me bad, can't be like the old days"—

TRACY: But that's not the point of the play! That's not what this is about!

GABY: Answer me this: What if the wonderful couple from Ohio loses their money or starts to hate each other or one of them gets Alzheimer's—everything changes, and now they don't love her so much. What if she gets married, and they split her up from her husband just the way they did two hundred years ago? What if they whip her for reading a map or lynch her for seeing her friends?

JOE: I didn't write *Mandingo*. These aren't those kind of characters! If they did that to her, I'd make her leave!

GABY: Tell him some of their indignities, Tracy.

TRACY: Well, punishment was very creative—nostrils slit, unuseful bones broken, teeth pulled out, toes cut off—anything painful that wouldn't keep them from working. And of course you know it was against the

law for a slave to learn to read or to look a white person
in the eye? We had to look down all the time or we
were considered a threat.

GABY: Three-fifths of a person, Mr So-Called Rock!
Her people were tortured for hundreds of years—
you have no idea what they went through!

JOE: Everybody knows what they went through, come
on! How could we miss it? We've all been bashed over
the head since birth by fifty thousand books, movies,
and miniseries telling us how wretched slavery was 'til
everybody's practically in favor of it!

GABY: In favor of it? You are one young, repellent man.

JOE: But that's the point of this play—LaWanda's so
miserable in her present life she fantasizes back to the
worst period of her racial history and decides it was
better than what she's got right now. The point is
LaWanda's inability to cope with life—regardless
of race.

TRACY: Regardless of race? Then why didn't you make
it about a white girl?

GABY: Excellent point, Tracy!

JOE: What bud are you folks smoking? Where's the
conflict in a white girl deciding to become a slave?
Theres no drama, no risk—

GABY: No, but see, see, I like this idea, you could turn
this into a sort of quite exquisite political statement—
we need to take care of others. But you've got it all
wrong. Get rid of the rednecks, make what is her name,
LaWanda? Make it Wanda or Wendy and make her
white. A white woman learns about slavery firsthand—
now *that's* a play—and a part! How slaves live, eat,
sleep, suffer, suffer, how their masters beat them, and
so forth. They have to bring in the corn.... Now there's
a role. Could be very moving.

TRACY: Not exactly what I meant—

GABY: It would make a great play!

JOE: It would not—no bitches or sluts would come see it! And it's not the play I want to write.

GABY: How about this—keep her black but have her played by a white woman.

OZ: Gaby, in blackface?

GABY: No, no, she stays white, but you *tell* the audience she's black. Like *The Elephant Man*, played by a handsome young boy, you know, "Sometimes I think my head's so big because it's so full of dreams."

OZ: Gaby!

GABY: Actors should not be limited by race, gender, age, imagination, nationality, or any of the body prisons! African-Americans should be able to play Anglos, and Caucasian-Americans should be allowed to play them! And why shouldn't Latinos and Latinas and Chicanos and Chicanas be completely acceptable as Iraquis or Poles or Pacific-Rim-Islander-Americans; men should happily play women, women men, oldsters youngsters young as pups, and so on without limit! A great actor is a great actor, period.

TRACY: Yes, yes, of course we agree, but what about the one-sidedness of the play?

JOE: Whadda ya mean "one-sidedness?"

TRACY: Your darky volunteers to be a slave, which to you means an idyllic life talking to sheep and running her hands through spring water—

GABY: Now there I agree with Tracy one-hundred-fifty-one and one-half percent—there's no balance. You've got to show the negative side of something like this, too.

JOE: This is a play, not a newscast! A work of art is supposed to be biased! A play's gotta be passionate, and you can't have balanced passion. I mean, should Picasso have made a *pro*-Franco painting to balance *Guernica*? You think the audience has to be shown the positive aspects of witch-hunting to properly balance your beloved *Crucible*?

GABY: I don't like the way you said, "beloved."

TRACY: But you glorify slavery! The Civil War wasn't some kind of spa experience, and there weren't any Walt Disney plantations like yours, everybody one big happy family!

JOE: But that was her *fantasy* about the Civil War! Besides, there were plantations like that—

TRACY: Next you're going to tell us that some slaves needed their masters just as much as the masters needed them!

JOE: Some did!

TRACY: You're saying some slaves actually enjoyed being slaves?

JOE: Some *were* happy! I did research!

TRACY: What's your source material—*Gone With the Wind*? Or Vachel Lindsay! And where did you get that line, "At least we all had jobs?"

JOE: Louis Farrakhan! Direct quote!

GABY: I knew this play was anti-Semitic! You are a highly twisted boy, young man—a sort of cross between Uriah Heep and Jean-Claude van Damme.

OZ: Joe is very eager to get his play on.

JOE: Eager? I'm desperate, man! This is my *life* you're talking about, and you're treating it like a pair of socks! You've all lost the wonder that, hey, first, hey,

somebody *made* those socks, and they're amazing!
They're a great color, they don't shrink in the wash,
and not one of you could ever have made any pair of
socks, not one!

GABY: Socks? What is he talking about?

CLAIRE: Murky, highfalutin' similes.

TRACY: The play, Joe—

JOE: Oh, forget my play! I'll just go back to my garret
and rip my heart out, ventricle by ventricle.

CLAIRE: Ah, Christ on the cross, just where artists feel
most comfortable.

GABY: Where do you live?

JOE: Hand-to-mouth, eating scraps, sleeping with
worms—

TRACY: Come on, come on—

JOE: In a ten-by-fifteen loft in Hoboken. Yes, I do
carpentry, yes, I watch television news twelve hours
a day. And you know what else I do that's really
degrading besides writing? I mop out at the morgue
when I'm not baring my soul for you brownshirts to
stomp on.

TRACY: Oh, please...

JOE: That's it, send me away, send the poet back to his
cadavers! I knew I should have been a pianist!

CLAIRE: Orchestras have artistic boards, too.

JOE: Then I should have been a painter! No one
collaborates with a painter, no one tells them what
to do.

GABY: I hate painters. They never *listen.*

JOE: What I have to remember is it's me who matters,
not you! I'm the artist! I don't need you!

creative people

passion

TRACY: Oh stop it—there are thousands of you out there, and how many of us? Twenty?

CLAIRE: Quite invigorating dealing with creative people, isn't it—as long as you've got the control.

TRACY: Invigorating?

CLAIRE: Yes. You can spot it a mile away—whether they're any good or not depends on whether they're sufficiently selfish to shut others out so they can work—and obnoxious enough to shove their work in everyone's face despite its constant rejection.

JOE: Do you really think we're that bad?

CLAIRE: Not at all. Artists stand for something— unpretentious selfishness. Conservatism so intense it would bring Disraeli to his knees. Always puzzled me that they weren't all right-wing fascists, since that's how they deal with their work. And they do have an admirable potential for violence.

GABY: Violence is admirable?

CLAIRE: It's passion gone crazy and proof of life. I adore that about them. It's what I adore about America.

JOE: Are you one of those gorgeous Brits who'd rather lance the boil than soak it? Cut through the clutter and chaos with brutal insight and wit?

CLAIRE: Yes.

JOE: I knew it! Hey, would you like to go to a club later? Dance? Or the fights? I can get passes.

CLAIRE: No.

TRACY: Oh, stop it—nobody's interested in your white male testosterone—

(JOE *advances on* TRACY *threateningly.*)

JOE: And just what do you do?

ACT ONE

[handwritten: power in the theatre]

[handwritten: Tracy, 43 new A.D.]

[handwritten: playwright]

OZ: Tracy's the dramaturg here.

JOE: The dramaturg? So you choose what plays get done?

OZ: Not yet. Tracy filters them; Gabriella and I decide what gets done.

JOE: Just what the arts in America need—a bureaucrat to filter the thickmeat just in case our creations might accidentally have an impact on somebody's life! Tell me, what's the difference between you guys, the government, and a bunch of television execs?

TRACY: I also student teach at N Y U, and I'm going for my master's in the history of theater.

JOE: Oh, couldn't get into the *film* school, huh, Trace?

[handwritten: no fire]

OZ: Now just one minute, boy! You can say whatever you want on our stage, but you cannot disparage Tracy's devotion to this theater! She spends thirty-six hours every single day down here! She has no other life besides this theater, if I'm not being presumptuous, Tracy.

TRACY: You're not being presumptuous, Oz.

OZ: When I had my bypass last year, she ran this entire operation single-handedly, mounted the entire one-act play festival herself! She is a loyal friend, practically our daughter, and a dazzling administrator. Which is why Gaby and I intend to make her the new artistic director next year.

CLAIRE: You're both retiring?

OZ: Just have to send out the press release.

CLAIRE: And the plan is, Tracy will take over your role?

OZ: The youngest African-American woman to run a major not-for-profit theater in the land.

[handwritten: P.C. heaven]

Claire

CLAIRE: I had no idea your profile with the artistic community was so high, Tracy. Congratulations.

OZ: Absolutely. What do you mean?

CLAIRE: Well, our important theaters are all run by artists—actors, writers, directors—gives them more credibility with the artistic community.

OZ: *(Defensively)* Well, Tracy's written plays. Nothing produced, but she's well aware of the artistic process.

CLAIRE: Never been produced? Well, I'm sure they'll make allowances in this case. She has shown no lack of finesse with Joe Rock here.

JOE: Who are you? So beautiful... Wouldn't it be great if you were a lesbian. Who'd let guys watch. I'd give half my ribs to make clutching, passionate, skin-damp, vicious love to a lesbian.

CLAIRE: You'd be burned to a crisp. *(Meaning* OZ *and* GABY*)* I'm a friend of theirs. I run the Hazlitt Theater in London.

JOE: The Hazlitt? Another theater named after a critic? Oh, I see, you think they're all going to give you good reviews because you name a theater after them? Why don't you just call this place "The New York Times Theater"—then you'd always have the critic in the palm of your hand no matter who it was. *(To* CLAIRE*) Are* you a lesbian?

directive

TRACY: Focus on the play, Joe—

CLAIRE: Why do men find lesbians at play so sexually exciting? Women don't find gay men sexually exciting. I'm unavailable to you, if that's what you're asking. Do all playwrights in your country write plays just to get laid, Oz?

OZ: Don't be naïve, Claire. Aeschylus wrote plays just to get laid.

CLAIRE: Might be quite fun to run a theater in America. Rather intense, but certainly keep one alert.

OZ: Really? You'd consider running a theater here?

CLAIRE: Well, it is still Mecca, isn't it.

GABY: You should hear Claire's plan for the Hazlitt. Tell Tracy, Claire.

CLAIRE: Not so much a plan as a dream, really. Long been a fantasy of mine to have a place in the country where all the artists could live—writers, actors, directors, designers—where honest work could be done without the competition and stress of London.

GABY: Doesn't that sound exciting, Tracy? Maybe you could do it—the Berkshires and Bedford are underpriced—

TRACY: Sounds a little impractical to me...and just how high is your profile with the artistic community?

OZ: Oh, Claire's won two *Evening Standard* awards for her directing.

CLAIRE: I try to keep the odd hand in.

OZ: Well, what's your take on this *Stonewall Jackson*?

CLAIRE: Well, as a foreigner, I may be totally off base here, but I think if you put this on you'd be lynched. Though that, of course, is not reason not to do it.

GABY: Really...

CLAIRE: There is a small matter of moral dishonesty, of course. But the chief problem I see—through years of running my own theater—is one of public relations.

TRACY: What moral dishonesty?

CLAIRE: Well, the whole crime of your peculiar institution—whether slaves were treated badly or

Claire's analysis

not—was that they had no choice in the matter.
And the girl in your little play does have a choice.

OZ: That is so perceptive!

GABY: What public relations problem?

CLAIRE: Well...here you have a white male playwright...
writing about—and demeaning—a black female...

OZ: Oh, my God, oh, my God, of course...oh, my God...!

GABY: We'd be excruciated! Ostracized!

OZ: Oh, my God, my God, let me clutch my head.
They'd hang us out to dry....

TRACY: But you knew all along he was a white boy!

racist play

OZ: Al Sharpton and the boys'd be down here with
fifteen cameras in five minutes!

JOE: You mean if it were written by a Guatemalan
señorita you'd put it on?

minority

GABY: We've never had a Guatemalan playwright.
Probably make the short list. That, you see, would
give it resonance. A racist play written by a minority.

JOE: Well, get out the burnt cork, folks, I'ze a white boy!

OZ: That's right, this is out of the question. We gotta get
moving, Tracy, only an hour and a half left—

TRACY: Joe—

JOE: That's it? You're throwing me out because I'm not
Guatemalan? Well what do I care—my life is over, my
career is dead! Where can I get a six-pack? I'm going to
get beer. Beer. So much beer, I'll float back to Hoboken!
Did you know this week it cures cancer? And you petty
dictators—I'm sorry people don't exist as you hope
they do, I'm sorry everyone isn't admirable and
sympathetic, but as long as you demand sentimental
and platitudinous mendacity, all the arts in this country

will always be a hypocritical foundry of lies! May all
you playground bullies be burned to death on the pyre
of your own piety, aflame in the bowels of your own
spirit-crushing megalomania! *(He starts to exit, stops.)*
Unless, of course, you wanted me to make some changes.

goes too far?

TRACY: *(Astonished)* Changes?

JOE: *(Hustling)* I mean, suppose, instead of having such
a demeaning job as tour guide, LaWanda was—hold
on—a lawyer.

TRACY: What?

GABY: Go on...

JOE: She hasn't won a case in twelve years, because the
criminal justice system is rigged against her. So the
Goshens are her new clients—

TRACY: *(Seething)* What are you talking about?

JOE: Just hear me out on this, Tracy. The Goshens are
her new clients and decide to retain her as head of
their legal staff. Change him from a folksy insurance
salesman to head of a racist corporation. Like Texaco!

GABY: Right on!

TRACY: Stop it, Joe—

JOE: I extend the play into two acts, and the second
act takes place in the Goshen's corporate headquarters,
Oklahoma City or wherever Texaco is, and a contrite
Barney apologizes to his wife for the years of
oppression and gives her the keys to the business.

TRACY: STOP! STOP! KEEP YOUR MOUTH SHUT,
STOP TALKING RIGHT NOW!

JOE: But...

TRACY: NO ONE'S MAKING ANY CHANGES IN
THIS PLAY WHATSOEVER! NOT A WORD, NOT A
COMMA, NOT AN INTERABANG! Except the author.

9

OZ: Except the author? Who do you think were talking to?

JOE: Don't do this to me, Tracy.

TRACY: Ladies and gentlemen, I hadn't planned it this way, but now is as good a time as ever. Joe Rock did not write *Stonewall Jackson's House*.

OZ: What?

GABY: What are you talking about?

CLAIRE: Really...?

OZ: He didn't write this play?

TRACY: No.

(This sinks in for a moment.)

GABY: Well, who did?

(A beat, then...)

TRACY: I did.

(Blackout)

END OF ACT ONE

ACT TWO

Scene One

(Setting: The Rehearsal Room)

(At rise: TRACY, GABY, OZ, CLAIRE, *and* JOE *are frozen in the same positions as they were at the end of ACT ONE.)*

GABY: Tracy!

CLAIRE: You wrote this?

OZ: Wait a minute, wait a minute—you wrote this play...he didn't?

TRACY: Joe Rock doesn't even like this play—

GABY: What?

JOE: I hate this play! Everything I've ever stood for, my middle-class upbringing, my tortured adolescence, every political stance I've ever taken, I have always embraced people of color. I'd be a member of the A C L U if I could afford the dues! Please don't judge me, everybody!

CLAIRE: I've never heard of such a thing...

OZ: You're a...a front for Tracy?

GABY: I haven't heard the word "front" since the blacklist...

CLAIRE: How Byzantine! But who are you then?

Neal Rellini

JOE: Just an actor. You have seen me before, Gaby. With a beard. I auditioned for *Breakfast Resonance*. Didn't get it, of course, but we met, and—

GABY: I knew I knew that voice! You're...you're—

JOE: Neal Rellini. Maybe you saw my Edgar in the Park, the coked-out punk in *Douglas Fir* at Playwrights Horizons, I've got that Coffee Tree commercial running—

OZ: I feel completely tricked—made a fool of!

JOE: It wasn't my idea. Tracy promised me I could play Junior if you did it, be on the regular audition list next year—

GABY: Tracy, how could you?

CLAIRE: You actually...rehearsed all that?

JOE: Yeah, by attacking her own play she thought Oz would defend it and become more convinced to put it on. I've got to know—does everybody hate me?

TRACY: Only those who know you.

JOE: She said, "Attack anyone you want, I'll protect you." I didn't want to, Gaby, not you and Oz in particular. I have so much respect for everything you've—

TRACY: Oh shut up, you pussy.

hoax

GABY: This is the most shocking literary hoax since Clifford Irving tried to smoke one by us with Howard Hughes!

JOE: She told me what to say when you called me a racist and how she went down to Virginia and saw this girl—this woman—and she told me to get mad when you brought up nontraditional casting. But there I drew the line!

GABY: And you told him the Louis Farrakhan thing?

Tracy - Play is about being indentured to a welfare state

TRACY: Yes.

CLAIRE: Well, I have to say, on the basis of his performance this afternoon, I'd hire him for anything he wants to play. Brilliant.

JOE: Yeah?

CLAIRE: Don't get any ideas. I only hire actors, I never date them.

JOE: How come?

CLAIRE: They steal the light.

OZ: Well, yeah—you were damn good.

JOE: Oh, thanks, Oz. I mean, it wasn't like all scripted you know—most of it was my own improv.

GABY: Very believable.

CLAIRE: And about me?

JOE: That wasn't acting. That was inspiration. My muse really kicked in there.

TRACY: Oh, anybody can act with a hard-on. Once this boathead started believing he actually wrote it, I realized we were tiptoeing into Lithium County. He couldn't keep his face of out the British vixen's lap, and he kept getting the point of the play wrong!

JOE: I did?

TRACY: Yes! It's not about wanting a welfare state— I told you that. This play is about us being indentured *now. To* a welfare state.

OZ: I just...don't believe it.

TRACY: Don't you see? We're just as indentured now as we were then—and it's precisely because of Claire's smug but unperceptive observation that it's so reprehensible: We do have a choice now, and what we've chosen is to be unbeaten, voluntary slaves.

New owners of Blacks

_52_   STONEWALL JACKSON'S HOUSE

CLAIRE: Smug *but* unperceptive? I should have thought it would be smug *and* unperceptive.

TRACY: You'll never get this place.

CLAIRE: And you'll never get to heaven.

JOE: That's why I kept gagging—I had to keep saying these vicious lies about African-Americans wanting to go into bondage! I just couldn't say it again with any integrity.

TRACY: No disrespect, Gaby, but over the last thirty years we've had more time, energy, good will, and money dumped on us than all the assets of the Fortune 500! And what did we get out of it? *New owners!* Instead of belonging to plantation fat cats, now we're the property of the United States Government and the Civil Rights Industry, Inc. You said you wanted controversy in the theater, Oz. Well, lookee here.

OZ: *(Flustered)* Well, yes, but by controversy I meant something like...like that picture of Jesus Christ in the glass of urine—

TRACY: Oh, Oz, the piss-Christ was out-of-date protest ten years before it happened. Who'd that offend— two nonagenarian Southern Senators and the Pope? Criticizing the Catholic Church stopped being dangerous in 1951. *This* is dangerous.

CLAIRE: Something I don't quite get. Why did you need him? Why didn't you just write the play and submit it under your own name instead of going through this elaborate charade?

TRACY: Every play I've written here gets a "Very exciting, dear, some of it is really quite innovative" brush-off. And then you tell me, "Please, please find us a playwright of color or we'll lose that damn grant". Hey, *I'm* a playwright of color! I had to show them how alive the play is without their knowing I'd written it.

GABY: Tracy, you didn't need to do this. We would have told you what we thought!

OZ: We're known for our candor!

TRACY: All right, tell me now.

GABY: *(Thrown)* Well...well...it's, uh, extremely interesting—

OZ: *(Helping her out)* —Rather bold, very exciting—

GABY: —Parts are very innovative...really makes you think....

TRACY: Exactly.

JOE: She wanted me to come back in later all drunk and criticize the next play you're reading. I drew the line!

GABY: *The Sweetness of Sammy Sadd*? I thought you liked that one—

TRACY: "You wounded me, Pop" "Wounded you, wounded you, son? Oh son, whadda ya, whadda ya—" "Oh, Pop, whaddo I, whaddo I?" Not a complete sentence in the entire play.

GABY: It is the poetry of the inarticulate.

TRACY: A father comes to grips with his gay son one neverdawning night over a bottle of Scotch.

GABY: We feel it has a shot at the Pulitzer.

TRACY: I'm sure it does.

JOE: She said you'd decide it was terrible compared to hers!

GABY: Tracy, that is despicable! Trashing another writer's work for personal gain!

TRACY: Yeah, like I'm the first one ever to do that....

OZ: I...I...just don't believe it....

TRACY: *(Furious)* I want the job! Now do you believe it?

(A moment while this sinks in. GABY *sees* TRACY *clearly for the first time.)*

TRACY: I got so sick of reading all those self-pitying *mea culpas* we get over the transom about how we been wronged. I mean, we *have* been wronged, but it's over, folks. Or worse, all those fake "I am a proud dyke of color and some kind of indomitable." Isn't there anything else to say about us? Are we forever to be defined by slavery and Jim Crow? That just makes us look wretched, like a permanent class of psychiatric patients. "Hey, we went through slavery, we went through Jim Crow, we gotta be dysfunctional." I want to change that, give us a new identity! I want to change this theater, change the culture, change the world! Shake things up—just like you, Oz. I know you'd be more confident in my being artistic director if one of my plays had been produced—well, produce this one. This is what I want the Macklow to be in the next century— a place that makes people think!

JOE: Oh, God, I am so loathsome, so swinish, a complete and total fishspine! How could I sell out the very things I've believed so passionately my whole life? I've gone against everything I've ever believed in. Won't somebody please hold me?

TRACY: Jesus, my casting sucks. Send out for Mickey Rourke, and I get back Richard Simmons.

JOE: Gaby, Oz, I was actually getting sick—I just couldn't say one more word about people of color begging to be slaves! No one would ever beg to be a slave!

TRACY: *(Turning on* JOE*)* You know what slaves found? The one percent who fought back got beat least!

JOE: Yeah, so?

TRACY: So that leaves the ninety-nine percent who didn't fight back. They had to get along somehow. You think there's no complicity in subjugation? Try this!

(TRACY *whips off her belt, loops it around* JOE's *neck like a dog's leash, and shoves him onto the floor. The others are stunned.*)

OZ: What are you doing?

GABY: Tracy—!

TRACY: Taking responsibility for your life—just like Barney Goshen. (*To* JOE) How do you feel?

JOE: Scared shitless.

(TRACY *kneels and affectionately musses* JOE's *hair.*)

TRACY: (*Seducing him*) Of course you do, what am I thinking? Just let me calm down for a second. Oh, Joe—Neal—what would you like to be called?

JOE: Well, I'm actually sort of beginning to like Joe Rock.

TRACY: Killer name—very strong. Very you. I'm not going to hurt you, Joe. I want to comfort you. You did such a wonderful job, see how you impressed all these important people? Do you think you could help me out just one more time?

JOE: You're not mad?

TRACY: I got a little upset when you started making changes in my play, but I understand how hard it was for you. I'm really incredibly grateful for your performance. You were so good we could have gone on for hours!

JOE: Oh, thank you, Tracy, thank you! And I can still audition next year?

TRACY: I gave you my word.

JOE: What would you like me to do?

TRACY: Just an acting exercise. Put this back on.

(JOE *closes his eyes, and* TRACY *leads him around by her belt gently.*)

TRACY: Close your eyes. Follow me around. Now heel...sit..lay down...play dead...how do you feel?

(*She plays dog tricks with him—roll over; beg; play dead. She tosses him an invisible treat. It's quiet and playful.*)

JOE: A little nervous.

TRACY: (*Kneeling and caressing him*) Of course. But it's sort of fun when the threat's gone, isnt it?

JOE: Well...yeah...

TRACY: Kind of liberating?

JOE: Yeah...a kind of very nice sort of surrender.

TRACY: You're a very trusting person, Joe. I love that about actors. Not so bad having your life defined by someone else, is it?

JOE: (*Luxuriating*) I have friends who'd never want to take this off!

TRACY: (*Softly*) That is so sweet! Oh, I'm going to take such care of you next year, Joe. Six productions...won't it be nice to have your rent secure? No more morgue... move into Manhattan? All tension vanished... uncertainty gone.

JOE: Ohhh...ohhh...

TRACY: You'll be appreciated at last, just as your friends've told you you should be....

JOE: Mmmmmmmmmmmmmmmmmm...

GABY: Claire, you're breathing through your mouth.

(*An excited* CLAIRE *blows down her blouse.* TRACY *rubs* JOE's *thigh.*)

TRACY: Just give yourself up to a greater power, Joe. No decisions—like a Charismatic or a Shiite. Always know where you stand, what your place in the world is. Isn't it safe?

JOE: Mmmmmmmmmmmm...

GABY: This is obscene. Pornographic!

TRACY: *(Holding out her belt)* Anybody else want to try this? Oz?

OZ: No, no, I'm a director. I do that master-slave thing all the time.

TRACY: Fergie?

(CLAIRE shakes her head, "No".)

GABY: *(To JOE)* Get up! Have you no self-respect whatsoever?

TRACY: Yeah, but see how seductive subjugation can be? In my play, LaWanda makes it clear hers is voluntary. She is seduced just the way we've been seduced!

JOE: You mean this was all just to prove some racist point in your play?

TRACY: Victimization is always at least somewhat voluntary. Isn't that worth putting on a stage?

JOE: *(Exploding)* You just humiliated me again!

TRACY: Well, yes.

JOE: You can't equate one minute of sexual titillation with two to three hundred years of enforced bondage! I don't want to be anyone's slave, and I don't want to be anyone's owner, and maybe youre some kind of professional victim, but, hey, baby, I'm not. In real life slavery isn't voluntary!

people like being told what to do

GABY: Of course you have grievances, Tracy dear, many, many grievances, but you're not really a slave—

TRACY: Look, it's easy to call Hitler and Mao and Pol Pot butchers, but they must have offered something in return or they wouldn't have been in power so long—safety, national pride, a better future. One man can't do it alone. "S and M" is never referred to as just "S." You have to believe either there's something inherently subservient in some human beings or that these systems actually offer payoffs pretty beguiling to both sides.

GABY: You have no idea what you're talking about with Hitler! He had guns, the police, the government on his side!

TRACY: I'm not saying I want it that way, I'm saying it *is* that way. Why are you all too frightened to at least ask why enormous numbers of people like being told what to do?

JOE: Boy, they'd love you over at *The American Spectator*.

OZ: I don't think I like this play.

Oz changing mind doesn't like it

TRACY: Oz, how can you say that? You were so eager to direct it! I saw you skipping in the hall on your way to rehearsal! You told me you were going to surprise and thrill us—

OZ: I think you misunderstood what I meant by "controversial"—

TRACY: Don't you remember all those things you told me over drinks at Sabu's night after night? "If Marx were alive today in America, he'd say it's not religion that's the opiate of the people, it's the arts!" Don't you remember saying that? "The chief responsibility of the artist has become to not hurt anyone's feelings." And you weren't drunk. Our audience needs to be stirred up—that's what you said!

arts as sedative

GABY: What you don't seem to understand, Tracy, is that audiences don't really like controversy. Unless they agree with it, of course.

OZ: Well, I meant something else—

CLAIRE: Tracy, surely you've been here long enough to distinguish between after-hours rhetoric and public policy.

TRACY: (Exploding) That's not what you said, Oz! You said you wanted to blow the roof off the theater—off all culture in the country! I said, "But what about Gaby, she doesn't want to blow the roof off the theater, she wants to do *The Sweetness of Sammy Sadd*, how will you get it by her?" And you said, "Tracy, if only somebody would give me the ammo, I'd not only stand up to Gaby, I'd make that bully fall to her knees!" You said!

GABY: What?

OZ: Never did!

TRACY: Yes, you did!

OZ: Did not! After what she and I have gone through all these years, you think I'd say something like that about my own wife? (To GABY) I never said that, dear. You're not a bully!

GABY: Of course you didn't. Or if you did you didn't mean it. We all have to vent from time to time.

OZ: Tracy, I just got this whole thing wrong.

TRACY: No, you didn't, you got it right, or nearly right, you were so brave about it! But you're caving now because you're afraid—

OZ: I am not "caving!" It really, really went right by me—

GABY: It's all right, dear. You're on the right side now.

OZ: Thank you, dear.

TRACY: *(Exploding)* Oh, you've never been on the right
side of anything, either of you, just the comfortable one!

OZ: What?

GABY: Excuse me?

TRACY: Sentimental, self-centered Old Lefties whose
well-meaning, stubborn politics have wrecked this
century—trying to stuff real, complicated anguish into
simplistic theories!

GABY: What real, complicated anguish?

TRACY: All of it! Racism! Welfare! Nam! Stalin!

GABY: Stalin?

TRACY: Yes, even him! You were told and told what he
was doing and refused and refused to let the sunlight
in even when it pierced your bulletproof sunglasses!
While he murdered and tortured more of his own
citizens than Hitler and Pol Pot and Idi Amin
combined, you protected yourself with lies so you
wouldn't have to admit you were wrong—and instead
focused on a bunch of mediocre move writers martyred
by a blacklist!

GABY: They were not mediocre writers!

TRACY: Well, mediocre martyrs then. I mean, what was
your response to finding out about the gulags? To turn
Solzhenitsyn into a crackpot for exposing them and
ruining your lives?

GABY: He is a crackpot!

TRACY: Of course he is—he broke your heart! Well,
it's about to be broken again.

GABY: Oh really? By who?

TRACY: By me! You and you Upper West Side reformers
were told and told just passing laws wouldn't eradicate
racism, but you wouldn't listen and when racism didn't

go away, you buried your head in the sand and said,
"I dont get it. Why aren't they happy?" Your noble
theories don't have anything to do with real life. They
are just as distant and idiotic as nontraditional casting!
I mean, face it—nobody believes men playing women
except in Vegas, and women playing men is just silly.

GABY: Not silly and completely believable!   = Same

TRACY: It's saying everybody's not only equal, they're
the same! Theory!

GABY: What's wrong with theory? Really, dear, didn't
you take *any* Black Studies in college?

TRACY: I wasted two entire semesters sleeping through
that baloney—never heard so much made-up history
in my life. That's all they teach in there—fictions about
our past supposed to make us feel better and self-
esteem exercises straight out of Big Sur. Spend hours
lecturing about the greed of your slave traders—and
none at all about the greed of our homey chieftains so
eager to sell us. And in the end if you have the nerve to
praise Booker T Washington instead of W E B DuBois,
they give you an F.

GABY: I had no idea you felt this way about things,
Tracy.

TRACY: I'm afraid there are lots of things you have no
idea how I feel about, Gaby. 'Cause you look at me and
all you choose to see is a child of racism. What if I'm
more than that? What if I'm less? What if maybe I ain't
black after all, ever think of that?

JOE: What the hell does that mean?

TRACY: Perhaps I don't fit the code. You can't be black,
if you date somebody white; can't be black if you don't
blame all your problems on racism; can't be if you think
some of our brothers in jail actually belong there; and

you can't *no way* be black if you don't see that Clarence Thomas has two heads.

GABY: *(Coldly)* Tracy, dear, you are about *this* far from crossing a very precarious line.

JOE: I've never heard such blatant racism in my life!

TRACY: Your idea of a racist is anyone who won't spend twenty-four hours a day fighting for our God-given right to get free handouts from the government—

JOE: Racist!

TRACY: Why is everyone who doesn't want to give us things a bigot?

JOE: Racist!

CLAIRE: Your constant use of the word "racist" is really quite a brilliant rhetorical device—anything troublesome can be dismiss by calling it racist; the other person stands paralyzed with fear, defeated, his career and argument in tatters. Quite like being one of your Salem witches, or a Lutheran in 1520, isn't it? You've successfully trivialized the word into meaningless.

OZ: Racist this, racist that. I don't even know what the hell it is anymore. Nobody does.

GABY: I'll explain it to you after six.

OZ: Used to be so clear-cut: slavery, lynching, people as property. That's racism! Can't vote, segregated schools, stupid rules about drinking fountains—*that* was racism. But now...what is it exactly? A taxi won't pick you up? You get a bad table at a restaurant? Somebody calls you the "N" word? Is this what all the fuss is about? Hell, they call me a Mick, I start laughing.

GABY: How long have you been camouflaging your feelings, Tracy?

TRACY: Since I've known you. I'm such a different person from who you think I am. You don't have a clue what's on my mind, and you never will, 'cause most every time I see you, I lie. Most black people do. We say what we think you expect; and every time one of us tries to break through and act like an individual, clang, you close the jail bars on us.

JOE: All they've tried to do with their whole lives is make up for everything done to you for the last three or four centuries.

TRACY: Well, please get them to *stop*. White people believe two things about race: one, that all people are created equal, and two, that blacks are inferior to whites. And now our massa-pleasing demagogues and your dilettante press have sprung to your aid, focusing on stupid distractions like reparations and was Beethoven black, theories about melanin dumb as phlogiston. I don't want reparations for some injustice done three hundred years ago! What if everybody demanded that? How far back should the blame go? Christians and lions? Ostrogoths and Vandals in 330 B C? "I'm an Ostrogoth, and I demand reparations for—"

JOE: Quit trivializing your own struggle!

TRACY: I'm not! You are! Quit giving us stuff!

CLAIRE: "Massa-pleasing demagogues"—interesting turn of phrase. Just who might they be?

TRACY: Why, the chief public relations arm for white racism—our very own leaders.

JOE: That's the thanks they get for trying to solve your problems?

TRACY: How can they solve our problems—they *are* our problems! Don't you get it? Listen. Everybody—regardless of race—is unhappy most of the time, for all

sorts of reasons, most of them having nothing to do
with race. But our loudmouth leaders want to simplify
the human experience by saying it's all because of
racism.

JOE: Wait a minute—you're saying racism doesn't exist?

TRACY: Of course, it exists. It's just that, in this country
anyway, it doesn't matter much anymore except to our
rabble rousers who'd be out of a job without it. If our
victimization-hustlers didn't play the race card, they
might actually have to be elected on merit.

JOE: So your leaders "fool" you into believing racism
matters? Horseshit!

TRACY: You saw the L A riots, didn't you? The night
less than a hundred homeys gleefully set fire to several
buildings, killing a few Koreans in the process? The
next morning a few thousand nonhomeys strolled
through a rather cheerful and clearly multiracial
shopping spree. The event resembled little more than
an extremely expensive college prank—we all saw
with our own eyes the fun everyone was having.

JOE: That wasn't a shopping spree! Those people were
furious!

TRACY: Oh, please—you saw their faces! That wasn't
anger, it wasn't revenge, it was exhilaration. Riots are
exciting—at least to the rioters. Imagine the adrenalin
pumped at the Boston Tea Party. And the moment
all the multiculturals finished picking up their new
appliances, you didn't see white folks or Mexicans
or Pacific-Rim-Islanders grabbing the mike. But *our*
glorious politicians practically tripped over each other
in their eagerness to tell the television cameras that
it was *our* riot. And thank God for the riots, so our
Maxines and Cecils and Godfather Jesse flying around
in some white man's plane could remind everybody,
"HEY! DONT FORGET US! WE GOT POLIO! WE

NEED MONEY! WE NEED PITY!" And Washington, duped again, clambered in like Pavlov's dog with its usual condescending bags of moolah, once again allowing our spokeshumans to explain criminality away with excuses of "black rage," when everybody could plainly see from the never-ending T V coverage that *(a)* most of the rioters weren't black and *(b)* nobody seemed particularly angry.

JOE: That's your take on the rebellion?

TRACY: Rebellion? Rouge it up anyway you want, it was a riot.

JOE: The white European male has had his thumb in your eye since 1607!

GABY: Now, that's true! No one has been tyrannized like women and African-Americans!

TRACY: Women? Women?! Who'm I supposed to feel sorry for first? All these complaints about a glass ceiling—anybody here have any experience looking at a *cement* ceiling? Yeah, yeah, women have gripes, too, but compared to what we went through it's Gripes LITE. Your suffering is to ours as decaf is to regular. "We could have painted the Mona Lisa if only they'd let us."

GABY: You have just crossed the precarious line, Tracy.

OZ: Is this some kind of Pirandello thing where it turns out this guy really *did* write this play and rehearsed you?

JOE & TRACY: No!

OZ: But, why are you so pissed off at your white sisters—you should be working together.

TRACY: 'Cause you need a bunch of guilty white men to make any progress, and there aren't too many of them left. "My white sisters" are splitting up the resources. Let 'em come up with their own agonies for a change instead of always stealing ours. "Well, actually, with a little imaginative use of metaphor, we've been slaves, too." Well, kiss my black ass, they weren't beaten, not like us, and they have never since the beginning of time for thirty seconds been a minority.

GABY: You're not only burning your ideological bridges, you are digging your grave.

JOE: Maybe affirmative action for some people is a bad idea.

TRACY: What's affirmative action ever done for us? One tenth of The Talented Tenth move into the middle class, and a couple of guys get to go to Yale. Yeah bo! All we ever got from affirmative action was bad publicity. White girls got all the jobs.

OZ: Look, godammit, everybody's had a thumb in their eye at some point! What about us? Do you know what the Irish endured during the years of slavery? We did all the back-breaking, life-threatening work that was too dangerous for Africans to do, because Africans were property, and Massa didn't want to risk damage to his property. But potato-eating Micks were completely expendable. For a penny an hour we did all the high-risk work sixteen hours a day until we were either buried or sent to the hospital or allowed to go home to four-foot-high, tin-roofed huts, eight to a room, with inside, open sewers and cholera seeping through the floorboards. The Eighteenth and Nineteenth Centuries were barbaric to everybody—but we didn't have enough angry historians, so nobody remembers what happened to us.

GABY: I don't want to get into competitive misfortunes, but you weren't actually slaves, dear.

OZ: Look, I know African-Americans had it rough, okay, but they weren't the only ones who did, and it burns my ass to hear all this sanctimony as though they

were the only people on earth who did! Burns my ass
when I see how far the Irish have come since then, and
the Jews, and the Japanese, and the Chinese for Christ's
sake, and the Scandinavians in the midwest, and the
French, the Germans, the Italians, Rellini—your people!
Even the goddam Spanish! And then how far you've
come! Your progress is appreciable only in the intensity
and volume of your complaint. I'm sick of it!
Everybody else has made America work for them
but you, Tracy. Everybody! Why?

GABY: Oz!

OZ: Oh, God, I am so sorry, Tracy, I—

TRACY: No, no, it's refreshing to hear you say
something you actually believe, Oz, though if I know
Gaby, you won't for long. We can't make America work
because we've been told since birth we couldn't hack
it—first by your people, now by our people. How could
we possibly function like normal human beings? We
went through slavery! How much longer are you going
to allow us to feed off our historic victimization?

OZ: You think all your political leaders do that?

TRACY: Not Dr King. He was the only one with vision.
He saw the long-term goal was harmony, not just
getting a lot of laws passed. He saw that *how* the laws
were passed were just as important as the laws
themselves. But, no, our hot-hormone boys opted for
their Raps and Stokelys and the most adolescent of
Mr X's many personalities and went around getting
everybody mad so they'd feel good for about five
minutes but lousy for the next two hundred years.

OZ: But what about all your mayors, governors, the
Black Caucus, look what they did in Haiti. Articulate,
powerful leaders—

Legcders
defend
Criming

Yes.
Self
involved

farty

TRACY: That's the trouble with you farty Old Lefties, Oz—you condescend to us by pretending rhymed couplets and rap slogans are powerful and articulate. Our leadership has no credibility, because they're too busy defending our criminals. They spend all their time making excuses for Colin Ferguson instead of bragging on Colin Powell. You ever hear white boys coming up with excuses for Gary Gilmore and Jeffrey Dahmer? Can you name a black astronaut? Most people can't name a black entrepreneur besides Famous Amos? Can you?

OZ: Well...uhh—

TRACY: Did you even know there were any?

JOE: Of course there are!

CLAIRE: Goodness, you people are self-important.

TRACY: *(Viciously)* What does that mean?

CLAIRE: You really haven't a clue, have you, that the rest of the world watches your age-old little dance with such amusement. You just go round and round, don't you, the Great White Father and his misbehaving adolescent. If you could get your head out of your own collective rectum, you might notice that there's much greater prejudice in almost every country in the world—and considerably less justice. The crimes that Arabs do to Jews, Jews to Arabs, Tutsis to Hutus, Brahmins to Untouchables—all are much worse than what goes on here. But you people are so self-involved, so self-important, your ingrown toenail becomes more critical than the rest of the world's terminal cancer. And since you own most of the satellites, we all have to hear about it!

JOE: At least we're working on it—

CLAIRE: But you're not working on solving it, you're working on keeping it going. Don't you see how you

Tracy — glad to be out of Africa

feed off each other? You *want* the dance to continue.
Without it, Tracy's right—your public figures would
have no employment—not to mention income. Without
the dance, you'd be like Europe now that the Soviet
Union's collapsed. There's nobody to be against.
That was part of Hitler's genius—and why Tracy's
politicians keep racism alive.

TRACY: Maybe we should pay reparations to the U S for
getting us out of West Africa in the first place.

GABY: How dare you say that! You think your
great-great-grandmother was lucky to come here?

TRACY: She wasn't. But I am. I've been to Africa.
Hated it.

JOE: Oh, I get it—you wish you were white!

TRACY: You're not just a knee-jerk, you're a full-body-
jerk. No, I am not a self-loathing nigger, and no, I don't
wish I was white. I wish I was more important than I
am—and I wish you'd do my damn play.

JOE: You wish you were a dead white European male.

TRACY: No, I wish *you* were a dead white European
male. And seventy-five percent of my wish has already
come true, so watch your step.

JOE: No, no, you hate yourself so much, you despise
everything about your own heritage!

TRACY: I do not! I just don't want to live in it!

CLAIRE: You seem to forget, Joe—or Neal—that
loathing one's own heritage was precisely what was
unique about the founding of your country. And what's
ironic is how much of your republic is now banding
together in separate, self-interested little groups which
romanticize the very customs and cultures they risked
their lives to flee. But don't you see, in two decades or
so the debate may not even involve Tracy's people: it'll

be over which four southwestern states to give to the Hispanics, or whether the whole month of Ramadan should be a federal holiday or just the feast at the end. Your citizenry seem intent on returning the United States of America back into the Squabbling Villages of Europe. Your goals, once the envy of the world, have deteriorated from daring and radical visions of unifying the planet into narcissistic little...dustballs.

GABY: (Indignant) Oh, really? And what are our goals now?

CLAIRE: Why, clearly, to be the best-entertained nation in the history of the world.

JOE: That is so kicking! Could we at least have dinner?

CLAIRE: Yes...but not together. The real villain of your Twentieth Century isn't Hitler or Stalin or Jesse Jackson or Gloria Steinem, it's Joseph Campbell.

JOE: Joseph Campbell—the myth guy? Why him?

CLAIRE: Because Joseph Campbell, in rebellion against his own Catholic upbringing, taught that each one of you is God—not an outside force—and he believed it right up until he died, when he chickened out and asked for last rites. Joseph Campbell and Luke Skywalker and Presidential adviser Anthony Robbins made it comfortable for you Americans to believe that the force was within each of you—and, therefore, that each one of you was the center of the universe. For all your religiosity, that's what you really believe, and that will be your ruin. No other country is so obsessed with obliterating spirituality and the presence of death with the trivialities of sport and show business.

JOE: That is so profound! What should we do now?

CLAIRE: Let your women run things for a while. Your men are all fagged out and deserve a rest. Thank them for twenty-five thousand years of faithful service, give *what to do*

them all cigars and melatonin and magazines and point them toward the pool. If that fails, reestablish the monarchy, that'd give you something to unite against. Perhaps have someone invade you—that always pulls people back together. And, Tracy, you can produce a prowar play about it when you take over the Macklow next year.

GABY: Assuming we step down.

TRACY: Assuming you step down? Gaby, for a full year you've been saying you were retiring at the end of this season! Just ten minutes ago—

GABY: What Oz said, and here I wholeheartedly support him, is that when he and I decide to step down, *that* will be the time to search for a new artistic director.

TRACY: But you said you were grooming me to be the youngest African-American woman to run a not-for-profit theater in the country!

GABY: But, Tracy dear, then you wrote this play...

TRACY: You mean...you might turn me down... because of this play?

GABY: Well, you meant what you wrote in it, didn't you?

TRACY: Well, yes, yes, but...

GABY: Well, you obviously have a strong creative drive, and what we really need is an outstanding administrator. Perhaps you should pursue your writing career.

OZ: Gaby—

TRACY: But Oz said I was a dazzling administrator!

GABY: Sometimes Oz gets a bit overzealous.

I will change script.

Can I

TRACY: Wait a minute, wait a minute, am I hearing this right? You're not only not going to do my play, you're going to can me?

GABY: No need to be melodramatic. Nobody's going to "can" you. I'm sure whoever takes over for us—Claire, for instance—would be happy to keep you on as dramaturg. Well, perhaps I shouldn't speak for her—

TRACY: Claire? But she's British!

GABY: That's racist, Tracy.

TRACY: But you said if this play wasn't written by a white boy, you'd do it, and it isn't, and it fits exactly into our mission statement of Vision 2000—

GABY: 2010.

TRACY: 2010.

GABY: I said if it were written by a Guatemalan, it would probably make the short list. Well, you're not Guatemalan, and the short list is full.

TRACY: Gaby, no—!

GABY: No, I'm afraid you can't unring this bell.

OZ: Can't unstir this porridge.

TRACY: *(Desperately)* Well, well, then I'll change it!

GABY: Really, how?

TRACY: *(Increasingly desperate)* Well, what if I, uh, made LaWanda more admirable, more sympathetic, just as you said, Gaby. She aspires to great things, but the world won't let her breathe, her folks beat her, she's a victim of society!

OZ: Now that's an interesting tack...

TRACY: I could get rid of those scenes where she's treated so well during the Civil War—no, better still, *clean up SJH*

keep the scenes, but what if the Confederate family tortures her?

JOE: More believable than what you've got now, but—

TRACY: I could cut the cast in half, maybe get rid of the rednecks altogether—

GABY: No, I'm beginning to like the rednecks—

TRACY: —or, or keep them, beef up their parts! Give them all dignity, make it a little less sitcommy and and—

GABY: Get rid of that lovey-dovey stuff between Stonewall and his wife.

TRACY: But they were devoted to each other!

GABY: Doesn't really work for me, though—

TRACY: Well sure, yes, yes, of course, that wouldn't be much of a change, do all that, and make it a little more like, a little more like—

OZ: Yes?

TRACY: —*The Crucible*.

GABY: Bravo!

TRACY: Cut out all the mean-spiritedness and the academic jokes, get rid of the anti-Semitism—

GABY: Thank God.

TRACY: Insist on nontraditional casting!

OZ: Well, we could give it another look...

TRACY: Think of the resonance the play will have, the actors' arcs!

GABY: I don't think so...

TRACY: BUT I'LL CHANGE EVERYTHING YOU WANT!! Why not?

Now Tracy is the slave

GABY: *(Thinking it out)* A little too insincere.
Too opportunistic, wouldn't you say, dear?

OZ: *(Uncertain)* Well...

TRACY: Please...please, Gaby...

GABY: *(Suddenly ferocious)* You liar! You coward!
Take everything we hold dear and shit on it! You little
thief in the night! Truth-mugger! Betrayer of my trust!
Dissembler! Fake! Ingrate! Slippery, ill-bred, self-
satisfied, condescending cunt! You have the hubris
to believe you can break my heart? You resentful...
whimpering...elitist! You think after this I'd let you
tear tickets at a theater I had anything to do with?

OZ: Darling—

GABY: After all we've given you! Took you on
vacations, showed you off to friends, confided in you...
and you trick my husband into turning against me in a
bar! A bar!

TRACY: I didn't, I didn't, no, Gaby—

GABY: Yes, yes, you didn't, you didn't. Solzhenitsyn *is*
a crackpot! *(Calming)* Maybe it is better if we let you go
now.

TRACY: No!

GABY: For the sake of the theater. Of all the arts.
(GABY dismisses her, turns away.)

TRACY: I'll never lead the life I dreamed of. I'm
shaking...my eyes are floating...I'm suicidal....

CLAIRE: Yes, you're quite like the guide in your play,
aren't you.

TRACY: But...but...I worked so hard...I've been such a
good girl...I thought I had crystallized our entire racial
predicament in twenty-nine pages. I thought this was a
Waiting for Lefty for the 90s...I thought you'd be thrilled...

T spinning

GABY: I am thrilled. Thrilled to see the self-loathing fascist you really are squirm before us. I won't pretend to know where we went wrong.

OZ: Let's get going! *(Yelling offstage)* Places for *Sammy Sadd!* We'll never finish by six.

JOE: *(To* CLAIRE*)* Look, just in case you take over, can I still audition for all the plays?

CLAIRE: Well, you *were* brilliant—

TRACY: But my heart is sinking, my head's all puffy, Gaby, you're spinning—

(Everyone ignores TRACY, *hurrying for the next play. Even* JOE *helps move chairs.)*

GABY: I'm leaving it to you, Oz—cut the next discussions short, or we won't even finish by seven.

TRACY: Little snowflakes in front of my eyes, Christmas songs, it was simple then. Momma, there's no floor under me, what should I do? I'll have no place to go, no reason to get up in the morning...what if all my friends liked me just because of my job?

JOE: *(To* GABY*)* I think that play about the gay guy and his father sounds fascinating!

TRACY: I don't have any friends outside of this theater! I can't just go to school, I can't stare at my walls. I'll wind up like Joe, spinning in a studio, sweeping up after cadavers. My folks'll say, "I told you so, serve you right."

*(*JOE *makes* CLAIRE *dance with him.)*

JOE: See?

CLAIRE: I do admire your persistence.

JOE: You can't be that busy later...

TRACY: Everybody always says, "Tell the truth," and when you do, they insist you compromise. But I did both!

CLAIRE: *(To* JOE*)* Well, maybe.

TRACY: I can't stand it, I'll lose everything—dreams, work, friends, the paltry salary I make here, everything! Am I really just wrong about the works? *(Suddenly shrieking)* Yahhhh!

CLAIRE: What is it?

TRACY: I'm so scared!

JOE: What of?

TRACY: We're going to die if you keep us trapped like this!

OZ: What do you mean?

TRACY: Where do we fit into all this? Are we just going to be a permanent beggar class living off your largesse? Fifteen I Q points—what if that's true? What if Claire's right—in twenty years we're no longer the most important minority? I mean, when all races are all over, cheek by jowl, and we're just a sidecar on your motorcycle—what'll happen to us? The Hispanics everywhere, Indians from India, the Chinese don't give a shit about us, and we know how the Japanese feel about a diversified culture! What'll happen when the Jews turn on us, and the grandchildren of the Baghdad Scud survivors become citizens, and the murderous Koreans— well known for being the most violent people on earth—what if they get to be...more? The *Timeses* of New York and L A, what if they turn on us, the networks, Larry King, all those women—

GABY: Not quite so arrogant now, are we?

OZ: She's trembling, Gaby—

TRACY: They'll all be so furious! And you won't let us out of the cage!

OZ: What are you talking about?

TRACY: Us! Me! The black American!

OZ: What about you?

TRACY: WHAT'LL HAPPEN TO OUR LEG UP?

GABY: (*Sudden revelation—sincerely*) Why, you poor thing! That's all we've been talking about all along.

JOE: Jesus, you poor kid, you're terrified.

(TRACY *is on her knees and shaking.* GABY *crosses to her, puts her arms around her to comfort her.*)

GABY: There's not going to be any revenge. We'll take care of you, Tracy. We always have.

OZ: (*Crossing to* TRACY) Is that what you're worried about? What kind of people do you think we are?

(CLAIRE *smooths* TRACY's *hair.* OZ *follows quickly.*)

CLAIRE: Come on Trace, pull yourself together. We're here for you.

JOE: She's freezing! Let me rub your hands, Tracy.

GABY: The human heart is most fulfilled when it forgives. (*They surround her, touching and holding her.*)

CLAIRE: You know, Tracy, I think your play is on a very grand theme. Brilliant, really. It just needs some rethinking, a little shaping. Perhaps we can help.

OZ: It's such a timeless subject...

GABY: Perhaps I overreacted. I do respect your passion, dear, misguided though it may be. But we've handled that before.

TRACY: We're only twelve percent....

GABY: That's why you need us to take care of you.

OZ: Open your eyes. We'll lift care from your shoulders like a cloak...

OZ, GABY, JOE, & CLAIRE: Mmmmmmmm...

TRACY: Who's we?

GABY: We. Us.

(GABY *puts her arm around* CLAIRE, *beckons to* TRACY. JOE *and* OZ *are left out and worried.*)

GABY: Oh, come on, Oz, Joe, you can be honorary women...

(JOE *and* OZ *cross to* GABY *joyfully, as if at the end of a very sentimental play. Arm in arm, they coax* TRACY *to join them. They hold this very pleasant tableau for a moment as....*)

(*End of Scene One*)

Scene Two

(*Fanfare!*)

(*A large mock* Playbill *flies in with the title and graphics for the play* The House of Mary Anna Morrison-Jackson, Survivor. *Across one corner a yellow banner reads* "PULITZER PRIZE WINNER!")

(*We hear the voices of the actors. The men play women and the women play men.* GABY *is* LEWALDO GAYLE, *a twenty-two year-old African-American male tour guide;* JOE *is* MAG NUCKOLLS; OZ *is* DEL GOSHEN.)

GABY: (*As* LEWALDO) (*O S*) And here we have the rotor ruffler of Ms Mary Anna Morrison-Jackson, Survivor, an item she loathed but which she was forced to use as a subservient female by her husband and tormentor, General Stonewall Jackson, domestic batterer and abuser.

OZ: *(As* DEL*) (O S)* Young man, is it true Stonewall
Jackson was killed by his own men?

GABY: *(As* LEWALDO*) (O S)* Absolutely not. He was
killed by his wife in self-defense. A close reading of
history by the scholars here at Ms Mary Anna Morrison-
Jackson, Survivor's house prove that Mary Anna
dressed up like one of his soldiers and set him on fire
while he slept, but that male historians thought this
made him a sissy and so invented the fiction that he
was killed by men.

JOE: *(As* MAG*) (O S)* Excuse me for interrupting your
powerful and convincing thesis, but I'd like to know
if that rotor ruffler is real.

GABY: *(As* LEWALDO*) (O S)* No, but it is the exact *kind* of
rotor ruffler that Jackson so savagely demanded.

(As soon as the actors have changed costumes, The Playbill
flies out, revealing GABY *dressed as a man in Nineteenth
Century overalls,* JOE *and* OZ *in* MAG'*s and* DEL'*s costumes
from Act One.)*

CLAIRE: *(As* JUNIOR*)* Oh, no, another fake! Listen here,
sonny. My name is Junior Nuckolls, Jr, and my wife
and me have come all the way from racist Southern
Georgia and even more racist Alabama, and there isn't
anything in this house that's authentic!

GABY: *(As* LEWALDO*) (Flustered)* Well, well, uh, we've
tried to make it look nice even if inauthentic, but—
(Aside) —oh, I am so distraught and alone!

OZ: *(As* DEL*) (Arm around* GABY'*s shoulder)* Are you all
right, lad?

JOE: *(As* MAG*)* Yes, I, too, wonder why you are so
melancholic, LeWaldo.

GABY: *(As* LEWALDO*)* It's genetic. As you know, it is
common knowledge that the chief cause of the Civil

War was the lack of self-esteem among the white male population of the time.

OZ: (As DEL) But how does this affect a virile African-American male youth like yourself, LeWaldo?

GABY: (As LEWALDO) Our scholars here at The Ibsen-like Doll's House of Mary Anna Morrison-Jackson, Survivor, have discovered that virtually every single American born before 1720 south of the Mason-Dixon line was a victim of child abuse.

JOE: (As MAG) Mercy!

GABY: (As LEWALDO) The Eighteenth Century Epidemic of Child Abuse caused the Nineteenth Century Outbreak of Poor Self-Esteem. This in turn caused a genetic orientation to warfare among men, and a genetic orientation to be date-raped among women.

OZ: (As DEL) Really...

GABY: (As LEWALDO) But here's the important asterisk: while the litigious gene was passed on to the men, it was NOT PASSED ON TO THE WOMEN.

CLAIRE: (As JUNIOR) So basically, LeWaldo, you're saying that the abuse of women and men in the Eighteenth Century caused a lack of self-esteem and a plethora of date rape in the Nineteenth Century, which caused the Civil War...because the women were not yet litigious?

GABY: (As LEWALDO) That's right. And had it not been for the perseverance of Mary Todd Lincoln and Julia Dent Grant, who planned the winning strategy of the last eighteen months—these United States of America would still be the Squabbling Villages of Europe.

OZ: (As DEL) Ah.

GABY: (As LEWALDO) And, because litigiousness is not genetic in women it explains why women have had to play catch-up in that area over the last hundred thirty years, and why they deserve larger settlements.

JOE: (As MAG) And that's why so many of us are looking forward to the Johann Sebastian Bach Retroactive Rape Trial.

OZ: (As DEL) What's the Johann Sebastian Bach Retroactive Rape Trial?

CLAIRE: (As JUNIOR) The Attorney General's final argument this morning left no reasonable doubt that the two Mrs. Bachs would never have had twenty children voluntarily.

JOE: (As MAG) But, the Attorney General didn't say it was because of Bach's cross-dressing—I mean that's genetic and hardly his fault.

CLAIRE: (As JUNIOR) In fact, it was used in his defense, and his estate may receive reparations.

JOE: (As MAG) But the rape evidence is clear and verified by Beethoven's European-Caucasian mistress in a letter written as she ghost-wrote his Seventh Symphony while Ludwig was away celebrating Kwanzaa.

GABY: (As LEWALDO) But even Bach's justified conviction will not transport my misery! (She breaks down and cries.)

OZ: (As DEL) Now, now, LeWaldo. We all feel your pain. My partner Barney and I have a beautiful resort in the free-thinking state of Ohio. Sometimes we take walks among the calming sheep and run our hands through the clear brooks burbling everywhere. How would you like to come back and live with us, and we'll take care of you?

GABY: *(As* LEWALDO*)* Oh, how my head swims in anticipation of your wooded offer! How trouble-free and race-neutral it sounds!

OZ: *(As* DEL*)* Barney and I will help you make up your mind about everything. You'll never want for food or money, clothing or friends or T V. You can stay as long as you want, go when you like...what do you say?

(A pin spot finds LEWALDO's *face. The rest of the stage is black.)*

GABY: *(As* LEWALDO*)* But, no, you want me to be your slave, Del Goshen, I can tell! Yes, I want to be protected from the cruelties of the world, yes, I want to be taken care of as in some welfare state—and Lord knows I deserve it after the millennia of racist, sexist, looksist, classist, homophobic, unfair shampoo and dry-cleaning oppression we males of all races have enforced—but what about my dignity? For I am a survivor just like Ms Mary Anna Morrison-Jackson, Survivor, and I need not your patriarchal suffocation, nor the attendant heartbruise and arrowsling! If it's the hatin', cussin' world versus your fascistic prison, I'll not the latter, I'll not the latter, I'll not the latter! Give me my earth and my freedom!

*(*GABY's *monologue concludes, and the pin spot fades. The unseen audience applauds and bravos wildly, then fades as country sounds come up.)*

(End of Scene Two)

Scene Three

(Lights come up on TRACY *and* CLAIRE, *facing D S in a line of rocking chairs. Next to them in the sunlight are three empty rockers.)*

sold out

CLAIRE: Sold out again, Tracy! What a glorious feeling. Isn't Bedford exquisite? Beyond my wildest dreams for the Hazlitt. So much excitement around your play, Tracy, *The House of Mary Anna Morrison-Jackson, Survivor*, all the awards, every major film studio bidding for it as a possible miniseries, two operas, *Time* Magazine's Person of the Year. You are the New Voice of the American Theater. Of all the arts, really.

(JOE *enters, kisses* CLAIRE *passionately. She kisses back. He takes the chair next to her and rocks.*)

JOE: Hello, darling. Seven standing ovations last night, Tracy. Congratulations.

(OZ *enters, crosses to a chair, rocks.*)

OZ: Seven standing ovations, Tracy. Unusual for a Tuesday. Joe, you were superb and Gabriella transcendent—her greatest role. So much dignity in it.

(*They rock in their chairs silently for a moment.* GABY *enters looking like Rebecca of Sunnybrook Farm.*)

GABY: Hello, everyone. Tracy. What a beautiful sunset.

OZ: Tracy agrees your performance was transcendent last night, Gaby.

GABY: Oh my God, coming from the playwright, the creator! Your play is so fulfilling—my crowning achievement, capping a lifetime in the theater. Oh. I'm so at peace here. The splendid isolation, the ice-sharp perceptions of art....

OZ: Yes, and I feel so safe. Safe as...you Brits have an expression for it, "safe as...?"

CLAIRE: Safe as houses.

OZ: Right. That's how I feel. Safe as houses.

JOE: So peaceful. Secure.

gushing (compliments

OZ: Sort of like a gentle rain on a farm somewhere in Ohio. Hey, look at that rainbow!

GABY: Know what I'd like to do after all this success? Just sit here and rock. Reminisce—but not about the past. We can reminisce about the future. I'm so optimistic! From here, it looks lovely. Clean and hopeful and bright.

(They stare at the sunset, rocking peacefully.)

(Slow fade to black—)

END OF PLAY

Tracy does not speak